RAISING

RELIABLE

REBELS

THE MAYA BECHI METHOD

MAYA BECHI

ROBSON & PURITAN
PUBLICATIONS

Cypress, Texas

TABLE OF CONTENTS

PROLOGUE

Parenting teens is often described as a balancing act, but in reality, it feels more like a tightrope walk or the dropped side of the tallest rollercoaster ride. On one side you have rebellion—their need to push boundaries, test authority, and explore independence. On the other side - reliability—their capacity to be dependable, responsible, and trustworthy. As parents, we often feel pulled between these two forces, unsure of how to reconcile them.

The truth is, rebellion and reliability aren't opposites. They're two sides of the same coin, and both are essential to your child's growth. Rebellion fuels self-discovery and

independence, while reliability anchors those qualities in responsibility and trust. Together, they shape the character of the young adult your child is becoming.

This realization became clear to me during a summer when my household transformed

from a calm and connected space into a battleground of shouting and slammed doors. My two teens, six years apart, had entered the turbulent phase of adolescence, and their once-loving dynamic was peppered with clashes and clap backs. I was caught between trying to rein in their rebellion and demanding reliability, and neither approach seemed to work. I was frazzled, overwhelmed with my personal grief and stressors from a divorce, new home purchase, and working two jobs.

Through trial, error, and countless reflections, I developed the framework that would become the Maya Bechi Method. It taught me how to embrace rebellion as a natural phase while nurturing reliability as a skill to be learned. This method allowed my family to move from chaos to connection—and now, I want to share it with you.

This book is your guide to navigating adolescence with purpose and grace. It's about turning the challenges of rebellion into opportunities for growth and teaching reliability in a way that builds trust and independence. Together, we'll explore how to transform this complex phase into one of the most rewarding seasons of parenting.

Rebellion in Adolescence

A Definition I like to use

Rebellion during adolescence is often misunderstood as defiance or disobedience, but at its core, it is a natural and essential part of growing up. Rebellion emerges as teens begin to

separate their identity from their parents and assert their independence. This phase is driven by developmental changes in the brain, particularly in the prefrontal cortex and limbic system. These changes heighten the adolescent's desire for autonomy, risk-taking, and exploration of new ideas, even if these behaviors conflict with established norms or parental expectations.

From a psychological perspective, rebellion often manifests as questioning authority, rejecting family routines, or aligning with peer groups over family values. While this behavior can be challenging for parents, it serves a vital purpose: helping adolescents establish a sense of self that is distinct from their caregivers.

Common Misconceptions

1. **Rebellion Equals Rejection**: Many parents perceive rebellion as a rejection of their values or love. In reality, it is often an effort to test boundaries and understand the consequences of autonomy.

2. **All Rebellion is Harmful**: While some forms of rebellion can lead to risky behaviors, others—such as questioning societal norms or advocating for causes—can foster critical thinking and personal growth.

MBM Perspective

The Maya Bechi Method views rebellion not as a problem to be solved but as an

opportunity to guide teens through self-discovery. Rather than suppressing rebellion, MBM encourages parents to channel it constructively by providing safe spaces for teens to explore their ideas and challenge expectations within supportive boundaries.

Reliability as a Character Trait to Be Trained

Reliability refers to the ability to be dependable, follow through on commitments, and act consistently with integrity. Unlike rebellion, which is driven by developmental exploration, reliability is a learned character trait. It is cultivated through repeated experiences that

teach responsibility, accountability, and the value of trust.

For adolescents, reliability is not innate—it must be trained through practice and feedback. This involves creating situations where they are given real responsibilities, allowed to face the consequences of their actions, and supported in learning from mistakes. Reliability also intersects with emotional intelligence, as it requires empathy to understand how one's actions affect others. Extending this type of setup/outcome/support opportunities is very challenging for most families. We like to rush in and absorb the impact, steam roll into a consequence, or cut the duration of an activity short because of impatience. The challenges have the potential to cause anyone to "pick and choose their battles". However, the benefits of truly going to battle (with a strategy) for every battle is so very worth it.

Common Challenges

1. **Inconsistency**: Adolescents may struggle with reliability because their decision-making skills are still developing, and their priorities often shift based on immediate gratification or peer influence.

2. **Parental Expectations**: Teens may resist reliability training if it feels imposed or overly rigid, especially during their rebellious phase.

The MBM frames reliability as a skill that should be nurtured rather than demanded. By entrusting teens with meaningful responsibilities and providing constructive feedback, parents can help them internalize the importance of dependability.

This process also

strengthens the parent-teen relationship, as teens see their parents' trust in their ability to grow and succeed outside of the home and in the community. This is a key segment and **do not skip this part.** The greatest influence at this point comes from outside of the home so the relationship you cultivate with your teen will be critical.

Connecting Rebellion and Reliability in MBM

At first glance, rebellion and reliability might seem like opposing forces—one driven by autonomy and risk-taking, the other by consistency and dependability. However, within the MBM framework, they are deeply interconnected. Rebellion creates the conditions for growth and self-discovery, while reliability grounds that growth in responsibility and accountability.

How MBM Balances the Two

1. **Challenging Without Condemning**: MBM encourages parents to embrace rebellion as a natural phase while setting boundaries that challenge teens to demonstrate reliability. For example, if a teen wants to challenge family rules about curfews, parents might allow a trial period where the teen is responsible for sticking to a later curfew and proving their reliability.

2. **Creating Safe Spaces for Risk**: By providing controlled opportunities for risk-taking—such as managing a household

responsibility or pursuing an unconventional hobby—the method helps teens channel their rebellious energy into productive outlets.

3. **Using Rebellion as a Teaching Tool**: When teens push back against expectations, the method suggests reframing the situation as a learning opportunity. For instance, if a teen refuses to complete a task, parents can engage them in a Socratic style question and space to determine the outcome options, consequences of their actions and how reliability builds trust.

4. **Reinforcing Positive Behaviors**: MBM emphasizes celebrating moments of reliability, even when paired with rebellious behavior. A teen who breaks a rule but admits their mistake and takes responsibility and meets the demands of the natural consequences, demonstrates both rebellion and reliability, which can be acknowledged as growth.

Practical Applications of MBM

- **Socratic Influence**: Use open-ended questions to explore the motivations behind rebellion and guide teens toward developing the practice of forward thinking to label how choices impact others and outcomes.

  Example: "What do you think it means to be trustworthy in this situation, even if you don't agree with the rule?"

- **Experience Learning**: Allow teens to experience the natural consequences of unreliable behavior while providing support to help them recover and improve.

  Example: If a teen neglects a responsibility, like forgetting to plan a meal, they might experience the discomfort of improvising dinner but also learn how to plan better next time.

- **Collaborative Identity Anchoring**: Frame rebellion as an expression of individuality while tying reliability to their role within the family and community.

Example: "I see that you're exploring new ideas, and I respect that. How can you balance that with the commitments you've made to us?"

Conclusion

Rebellion and reliability are not opposites but complementary aspects of adolescent

development. By embracing both within the MBM framework, parents can guide their teens toward becoming independent, dependable, and self-aware adults. Rebellion provides the

spark for growth, while reliability ensures that growth is grounded in responsibility and trust. Together, they form character development that prepares teens for the complexities of adult life.

INTRODUCTION

Understanding Adolescence as the Second Transition

Parenting adolescents can feel like venturing into uncharted waters, but it doesn't have to. I remember the moment I felt like the teens years were looking just like the toddler-to-child transition. The terrible twos, which were actually the terrible twos and threes for my household. During early childhood, this phase represents a significant period of growth and transformation. It's a time when little children crave independence, seek interdependence, and require structure and support to navigate emotional, physical growth and intellectual challenges. These years are pivotal, much like the "terrible twos"— only now, they're

expressed in bodies that match your size, complete with evolving worldviews and emotions that run deep.

My firsthand experience as a high school and middle school teacher with over a decade in

the job, I thought my professional background and parenting of my firstborn would give me an advantage. I did not feel advantaged. Then, I thought with confidence that the lessons

learned from raising one child could be applied to my second born. For the most part, I was wrong. My two children, six years apart, couldn't have been more different. Their attitudes toward friendships, school, and even family dynamics were vastly unique. Once puberty

arrived, these differences became more pronounced, shifting how they related to each other and to me.

What began as occasional disagreements between siblings quickly transformed, over the course of one summer, into a shouting household. Their once-adoring sibling bond was

peppered with hair-trigger clap backs. Previously cooperative, my teens suddenly became resistant to redirection and correction. It felt like I was parenting through the "terrible twos" all over again—but this time with individuals my size or taller. I was mortified and overwhelmed, questioning my ability to guide their choices and outlooks. I felt overloaded.

Life loads can come in a variety of demands. In a dysregulated world full of dysregulated people using the term dysregulation and other mental health buzz words, everyone is searching for something. We have lots of content from people offering advice, prescriptions and commands on how to solve personal issues and family problems. Nowadays you can find a how-to or life coach from anyone with a camera sitting in their car. In previous years, this was the scene in a barber or beauty shop, or at the kitchen table, or over a card game and a beer.

Life is changing. And you get to choose any method you wish to move forward in life as you navigate the second transition (teenage) years with your children. You may not be an expert in neuroscience, coping skills, or self-talk. You may not even know why you can't seem to stick to eating more protein and vegetables. You may be an expert in your field at your job, but the outcomes you want for your children seem elusive sometimes.

Let me assure you that you are, indeed, the expert on… you and your child.

Return to basics. Home. If home is not ok, then return back to you. If you believe that you are

not completely ok right now, let's begin by picking a space. Get focused. Give that one spot your presence. Although this section is about the teenage phase likening the terrible twos, I think it is a great time for me to mention you and recommend a big huge dose of self reflection. Are you surprised with this segue?

Consider, for a moment, my story:

It was just slightly past 5am on a dark Monday morning. Me, sitting half dressed on the floor of my walk-in closet with the edge of the hems of our clothes gently grazing the back of my head. Kneeling on all fours down on the floor, my face was so close to the carpet I could feel the puddle of tears and sweat slowly rising up off the floor to meet my nose as the wefts of carpet were filled by my outpouring. Mondays gave me anxiety. My common practice during these times was to have one good 30 minute cry early in the morning before my household was up. I'd say a prayer and then move into the rest of the morning routine. At some point there was a portion of my everyday life that felt out of my control and above my ability to bring it back to a manageable level.

The pressure to maintain personal or family schedules, the household duties, is real and necessary. If you don't take care of your space and home, who will? You still need to go to work everyday, or take care of parents, or manage multiple other household duties and functions.

When you set out to create a life for yourself you had goals and you have a certain portion of resources. You have a limited amount of energy to go after achieving all of these things.

Your story may not include daily closet floor crying sessions, but it may look more like:

-not knowing where to begin

-Frustration with the lack of task completion around the house

-Apathetic behavior or complete detachment from the day to day life at home

-A desire to have more than just work and falling asleep until the next time off (if any at all)

-Feeling like you have failed and lost control over your teenager and throwing your hands up

-Waiting for the positive outside influences to kick in (i.e. coaches, sports, mentors, school, etc)

Can you tell which of these describe the parent or the teen?

This is why adolescence is the "second transition." This is why the second transition is also a time for parent reflection and a return to a more teenage-like paradigm. This second

transition is not simply an extension beyond childhood where you can now make them do their own laundry and drive their siblings to a few activities so you can rest; No, it's a

pivotal phase with its own unique challenges and *opportunities*. And while it may feel overwhelming, you are better prepared than you think to guide your teenagers through this transformative stage.

Why You're More Prepared Than You Think

You live in the real world.

In the chaos of adolescence, it's easy to doubt yourself as a parent. Modern challenges like social media, academic pressure, and rapidly shifting cultural norms can make even the most seasoned parent feel like they're on shaky ground. But here's the truth: you've already been here before, in a way.

Think back to those early years of parenting when your toddler learned to walk, talk, and explore the world. You developed skills to create structure, set boundaries, encourage

curiosity, and provide emotional support. Those skills haven't disappeared. Adolescence is simply a new chapter where those same principles apply—this time with a more complex set of needs and a massive environment upgrade.

Outside.

Unlike the toddler years, however, you enter adolescence with an added advantage: experience. You've already honed your parenting instincts and gained insight into your

child's personality. You've seen what works, what doesn't, and how to adapt when things go sideways. While adolescence introduces new dynamics, you're no longer navigating uncharted waters—you're simply adjusting your course with the tools you already have.

The Maya Bechi Method™ (MBM) was born from this understanding. It's designed to

empower you to shift from controlling your child's behavior to facilitating their growth and independence. This isn't about micromanaging their choices or avoiding conflict; it's about building a home environment where they feel supported in exploring their identity and

equipped to make thoughtful decisions when they are not in your presence.

Parenting through adolescence is challenging, but it's also an opportunity to deepen your connection with your almost adult human, and prepare them for adulthood. Together, you'll not only survive this phase—you'll thrive in it!

Overview of the MBM

The Maya Bechi Method™ (MBM) is a practical, philosophy-driven approach with

actionable steps, designed to guide parents through the complexities of raising pre- and post-pubescent youth. At its core, the MBM embraces the adolescent years as an opportunity rather than a challenge—an opportunity to foster independence, strengthen emotional resilience, and deepen the parent-child relationship.

The method draws from three powerful influences:

1. **Socratic Philosophy**: Encouraging critical thinking through open-ended questions, helping you to provoke a deeper understanding and labeling of emotions, decisions, and personal or shared values. It also reveals the areas where values are diverging and your teen is establishing stronger personal convictions.

2. **Ancestral Wisdom**: Grounding family dynamics in shared cultural practices, storytelling, and traditions that have stood the test of time. A divergence in values can be anchored with the basic foundation of what connects you as family, thereby establishing a ground.

3. **Developmental Research**: Applying evidence-based strategies to support brain development, emotional regulation, and healthy decision-making.

What sets the MBM apart is its adaptability. Whether you've raised your child using a

specific framework like the Montessori Method or you've taken a more intuitive approach,

the MBM works seamlessly to meet your family where you are. It acknowledges that no two families—or children—are alike and provides tools to create a personalized parenting experience.

MBM doesn't aim to make parenting "easy" or eliminate the challenges of adolescence. Instead, it equips you to navigate these challenges with confidence, turning potential conflict into opportunities for growth and understanding. Through this method, your role evolves from traditional parenting to facilitation, collaboration, and training and empowerment.

The Three Core Components of MBM

The Maya Bechi Method™ is built on three foundational pillars, each designed to address the specific developmental needs of adolescence:

1. Pre-Taught and Experience Learning

In adolescence, much like in early childhood, learning happens both through direct teaching and hands-on experience. Teens NEED experiences. The MBM encourages introducing new concepts without pressure, allowing your child to explore ideas naturally. So, go for it. Set them up! The goal here isn't immediate mastery—it's planting seeds of curiosity and awareness that will grow over time.

- **Pre-Taught Learning**: Focus on introducing foundational ideas, like time management, ethical decision-making, or emotional awareness. These lessons are meant to be light-touch, sparking interest rather than requiring memorization.

- **Experience Learning**: Let your child experience the consequences of their choices in a safe environment. For example, if they forget to set a timer while baking, allow them to learn from the results without stepping in to "rescue" them. These moments teach responsibility, problem-solving, and self-efficacy.

2. Self-Directed Emotional Activity

Adolescents thrive when they're given tools to explore their emotions and regulate their feelings, but they also need guidance to develop these skills. Self-directed emotional activity is a collaborative effort, requiring your presence and consistency as they navigate this new terrain.

- **Emotional activities Include**: Cooking, physical exertion, meditation, breathwork, and emotional intelligence exercises. These activities not only trigger positive

- hormones like dopamine and oxytocin but also foster bonding, self-regulation, and self-determination.

- **Building Intentional Habits**: Start small, with activities lasting just 7 minutes a day, and gradually increase as your teen builds confidence and engagement. Eventually turn over whole portions of a week, a month, or a semester as they head towards a time when they will move out and become independent.

3. Collaborative Identity Anchoring

The teenage years are also a critical period for identity formation, and your role as a parent shifts from teaching to facilitating. Collaborative identity anchoring involves intentional actions to help your child explore who they are, where they fit in, and how they contribute to the world.

- **Practical Steps:** Include physical touch and real-world community activities to foster and develop and encourage connection.

- Facilitate decision-making and conflict resolution within the family and extend to the broader community or family members outside of the core home.

- Introduce digital resilience strategies, teaching your child to navigate online spaces with confidence and care.

Collaborative identity anchoring transforms the parent-teen relationship into a partnership, where you guide rather than dictate, and where your child feels supported in becoming their most authentic self.

CHAPTER

PART I

FOUNDATIONS OF THE MBM THE PHILOSOPHY BEHIND THE METHDOD

Ancestral Methods: Rooted in Culture and History

Parenting isn't something we're meant to do alone, and we're certainly not the first generation to face the challenges of raising children. I am personally reeling from how easy it was to move across the country to secure opportunities, but now it takes extra effort to

build community, connect with family and access support. Across time and cultures, families and communities have relied on shared practices, traditions, and storytelling to instill values, teach life lessons, and create a sense of belonging. These ancestral methods remain as relevant today as they were generations ago, even in a world of rapid technological and societal change.

One of the most timeless tools in parenting is storytelling. Stories carry lessons that go beyond lecturing or warning—they engage the imagination, evoke emotion, and leave

lasting impressions. Growing up, I had the privilege of knowing my maternal grandparents and my paternal grandmother, who were wonderful storytellers.

My grandmother told us about an uncle who went to a party and was never the same afterward. We'd always press her for details, and she'd tell the story slowly and deliberately, weaving in lessons about drinking, the risks of food or drinks being tampered with, and how substances can alter your brain and body. This story was unforgettable—it wasn't just a tale about Uncle J; it was a vivid, memorable lesson about substance use and vigilance.

I've since passed this story on to my teens, updating it for modern times. The message remains the same: be aware, make smart decisions, be aware of your surroundings and understand the potential risks of your choices. What makes these stories powerful is that they don't require perfection or endless detail—they just need to be shared. Whether the memories are good, bad, or somewhere in between, the value lies in the connection they create and the lessons they convey.

You don't need to have grown up with storytellers to incorporate this into your parenting. Start by sharing what you know—whether it's a family tradition, a memory, or a cultural tale. The goal isn't to craft a polished narrative but to pass down something meaningful, something your child can carry forward. Stories remind our children that they're part of something bigger, grounded in a shared history and a web of relationships that stretches across generations.

Practical Ways to Use Storytelling:

1. Share lessons from your own life or family history that align with values you want to teach.

2. Use stories to address current challenges your adolescent faces, connecting timeless lessons to modern scenarios.

3. Encourage your teen to ask questions about family stories, making it an interactive and engaging process.

Developmental Frameworks: Evidence-Based Practices

Adolescence is referred to as the "second infancy" because the brain undergoes significant remodeling, similar to the rapid changes that occur in early childhood. Understanding these changes can help you navigate your teen's behavior with more patience and clarity while giving you strategies to support their development effectively.

What Happens in the Adolescent Brain?

1. **Pruning and Strengthening**: During the teen years, the brain begins pruning unused neural connections and strengthening frequently used ones. This process makes the brain more efficient but also leaves it vulnerable to poor habits or decisions becoming hardwired.

2. **Prefrontal Cortex Development**: The prefrontal cortex, responsible for decision-making, impulse control, and emotional regulation, is still developing during adolescence. This explains why teens can struggle with planning ahead or managing strong emotions.

3. **Increased Sensitivity to Rewards**: The brain's reward system is highly active, making teens more likely to seek out novel and stimulating experiences. While this can lead to risky behavior, it also means they're primed for learning and growth.

Actionable Tips to Support Brain Development:

- **Encourage Routine**: Adolescents thrive with structure, even if they push back against it. I promise. Regular sleep schedules, mealtimes, and study habits help stabilize their still-developing prefrontal cortex. Bring back story time at bed time. It can be short, brief and powerful, or a cliffhanger, it really won't matter. It doesn't have to be bedside with a tuck-in. Rather, leaning on the counter while brushing teeth is also a great spot to insert yourself. In less than a week, you have a new trigger for requesting they get adequate sleep that doesn't sound like "go to sleep, get off the game, it's late." It can become "Did I ever tell you about the uncle who lost all of his money gambling?"

- **Standard Pediatrician Tip**: Aim for 8–10 hours of sleep per night, and reduce screen time an hour before bed to avoid blue light interference with melatonin production.

- **Provide Opportunities for Decision-Making**: Let them take the lead on age-appropriate decisions, such as planning a family outing or managing their own homework schedule. This helps strengthen their prefrontal cortex and requires forward thinking for an end time and practice with calculating when to return home. Curfew stories and the days of breaking them are always an easy win for demonstration sake.

- **Tip**: Start small—give them two or three options to choose from rather than an overwhelming blank slate.

- **Teach Emotional Regulation Tools**: Activities like mindfulness, journaling, and breathing exercises can help teens manage their heightened emotions. Often times structure and routines are more prominent with high stakes commitments likes sports. Their desire to win or perform at a level they dream of can catalyze them into a spiral of emotions and stress.

- **Tip**: Introduce simple techniques, such as the "5-5-5" breath (inhale for 5 seconds, hold for 5 seconds, exhale for 5 seconds), during moments of stress.

- **Model Healthy Habits**: Teens learn by example, so show them how to handle stress, solve problems, and maintain balance.

- **Tip**: Share your own strategies openly, such as how you organize your time or calm yourself when overwhelmed.

Research in Action:

We know that studies have shown that consistent sleep routines improve memory and emotional regulation in adolescents, while mindfulness practices reduce anxiety and impulsivity. By aligning your parenting strategies with these findings, you're not only supporting your teen's current growth but also setting them up for long-term success.

By combining storytelling, cultural connection, and brain science, you'll create a well-rounded foundation for parenting through adolescence. The next chapters will explore how to put these ideas into action, ensuring that you're equipped to guide your child through this transformative stage.

The Role of Technology

Technology is an inescapable part of modern life, and for adolescents, it's both a powerful tool and a potential source of harm. Screens, social media, and online interactions have become central to how teens communicate, learn, and entertain themselves. While these advancements bring many benefits, they also introduce unique challenges, especially for developing minds.

The MBM doesn't focus on restricting technology outright. Instead, it builds on existing research about screen time's effects on adolescents to create a balanced, intentional approach to digital wellness. By addressing the underlying developmental and emotional needs that drive excessive or unhealthy screen use, MBM offers strategies that are both practical and transformative.

Screen Time and Adolescent Development

Research has shown that excessive screen time can interfere with critical aspects of adolescent development. Studies like those from the American Academy of Pediatrics (AAP) highlight potential impacts, including disrupted sleep cycles, decreased physical activity, and heightened anxiety or depression. Adolescents' brains, particularly the prefrontal cortex responsible for decision-making and impulse control, are still developing, making them especially vulnerable to the overstimulation that comes with constant connectivity.

Building on this research, it is a key to note that not all screen time is created equal. Passive consumption, like endless scrolling or binge-watching, affects the brain differently than active engagement, such as creating digital content or using technology for collaborative learning. By distinguishing between these types of use, MBM helps parents guide their teens toward healthier habits.

Practical Strategies for Digital Wellness

The MBM approach to digital wellness emphasizes collaboration, self-awareness, and skill-building. Unlike existing methods that focus primarily on limiting screen time through parental controls or time restrictions, the MBM encourages teens to take an active role in shaping their digital habits.

1. Redefine Screen Time Categories

Inspired by research from organizations like Common Sense Media, MBM helps families classify screen time into three categories:

- **Passive Use**: Scrolling, binge-watching, or consuming content with no clear purpose.

- **Active Use**: Creating, learning, or engaging meaningfully online (e.g., making videos, coding, or participating in virtual study groups, art as therapy).

- **Necessary Use**: Technology used for school or work.

MBM Connection: By identifying how teens use screens, parents can work with them to set intentional goals for each category. For example, a family might decide to limit passive use while encouraging active and necessary activities that align with personal or academic growth.

2. Screen-Free Zones and Times

Building on the work of the American Psychological Association

(APA), which advocates for device-free family meals and bedtimes, MBM takes this idea further by integrating "screen-free rituals."

- Examples include nightly family check-ins, weekend hikes, or collaborative cooking sessions, nostalgic board gaming sessions—all designed to strengthen relationships without digital interference.

MBM Innovation: MBM emphasizes co-creating these rituals with teens, giving them ownership of the process. This approach builds trust and ensures the boundaries feel less like rules imposed by parents and more like mutual agreements.

3. Encourage Digital Resilience

Inspired by the concept of digital literacy, which teaches critical thinking about online content, MBM incorporates a unique focus on "digital resilience." This involves helping teens navigate the emotional and social challenges of being online, from handling cyberbullying to managing feelings of inadequacy stemming from social media comparisons.

- Activities might include family discussions about online experiences, setting boundaries for social media interactions, and role-playing responses to negative online encounters.

MBM Connection: The emphasis on emotional intelligence as part of digital resilience ties directly to MBM's focus on self-directed emotional activity. Teens learn not just how to regulate their emotions offline but also how to apply these skills in digital spaces.

4. "Digital Wellness Contracts"

Building on the idea of family media plans recommended by AAP, MBM introduces customizable "Digital Wellness Contracts."

- These agreements outline expectations for technology use, like limiting passive screen time to specific hours or prioritizing offline activities.
- Teens contribute their own goals and ideas, fostering a sense

of accountability and collaboration.

MBM Innovation: Unlike static rules, these contracts are revisited, negotiated and updated regularly, encouraging adaptability as teens' needs and interests evolve. This dynamic approach reinforces the philosophy of fostering independence through collaboration and training them to practice forward thinking and planning.

Connection to Core Components

The role of technology and digital wellness ties directly into all three core components:

- **Pre-Taught and Experience Learning**: Teach your teen about the science of screen time and its impact on their brain, then allow them to experience the benefits of balanced use. For example, help them set up a schedule to replace passive scrolling with active hobbies, like photography or music production.

- **Self-Directed Emotional Activity**: Use technology intentionally to support emotional regulation. Apps for mindfulness, journaling, or fitness can complement offline activities like breathwork or meditation.

- **Collaborative Identity Anchoring**: Help your teen create a positive digital identity by exploring ways to use technology for self-expression and community building.

  This might include starting a blog, learning to code, or volunteering for a digital cause or supporting younger children in the neighborhood or family.

Why This Matters

Technology isn't going away, and it's not the enemy. When used intentionally, it can be a powerful tool for growth, connection, and learning. The method equips parents and teens with strategies to navigate the digital world thoughtfully, ensuring that screens enhance rather than detract from their development.

In the following chapters, we'll explore more ways to integrate MBM principles into your family's daily life, starting with creating routines and fostering emotional resilience.

Preparing Yourself for the Journey

Parenting teenagers requires preparation and forethought—not just for your teen's development but for your own emotional readiness. Adolescence isn't just a transformative time for them; it's also a season of growth and adaptation for you. The emphasis on reframing parenting as facilitation and cultivating emotional fortitude, allows you to meet the challenges of this phase with confidence, clarity, and compassion.

Reframing Parenting as Facilitation

Traditional parenting often involves managing every detail of a child's life, from setting schedules to making decisions about school, extracurriculars, and household responsibilities. While this level of oversight is necessary in early childhood, adolescence marks a shift. Teens crave autonomy, and how you respond to this need can set the tone for their relationship with independence.

The Maya Bechi Method introduces a distinct approach to one of the biggest challenges of parenting adolescents: learning and practicing when and how to step back. Reframing parenting as facilitation means intentionally deciding which aspects of household life can be turned over to your teen's judgment and leadership. This is not about relinquishing all control; it's about giving your teen real responsibility in a way that meets their developmental need for autonomy while also helping them build critical life skills like decision-making, time management, and accountability.

My youngest is officially a teenager so I turned over our $100 per week grocery budget. I provided an 8 second overview of the meal plan for the week and she mostly ignored all of what I said and filled the cart with her needs. She focused on bottled water, items for daily school lunch and "good" breakfast items. I followed around behind her with a little bit of concern for my decision. Right before we approached the end of the aisle leading into the checkout lanes, she pause the cart, pulled out her phone and decided to calculate everything to check the total. She then turned to me and asked me what would we eat for dinner. Instead of saying "I already told you", I simply repeated what the meal plan was.

After she deliberated on if a week required the 24 pack of Z-bars, she tweaked the cart contents, collected a few vegetables and fruits and we made our way to pay. Since she was under budget, she asked if she could keep the money that wasn't spent. I agreed that at the end of the week, she could have whatever remained. The only caveat is that we need to eat. We pinky linked in agreement. To my surprise, the rest of my day with my 13 year old was pleasant, and filled with jokes. She thrives on feeling in control, but I also noticed that she was ignited in her nurturing side. When she was a little girl, giving her a dollar and allowing her to choose an item, graduates to her handling our nourishment for the week. Not because I couldn't do it, but because I trusted her and desired for her to take control with no mommy clap backs.

This approach recognizes that autonomy is not just a privilege but a developmental necessity. Research published in the Journal of Adolescence underscores the link between age-appropriate independence and stronger problem-solving skills, self-efficacy, and emotional resilience. Building on this research, the MBM emphasizes full delegation of specific tasks or responsibilities rather than partial involvement.

How This Could Look in Practice

One example of reframing parenting as facilitation is turning over the grocery budget to your teen for two weeks or even a full month. This task requires them to plan, prioritize, and manage resources—all essential skills for adulthood. Of course be prepared for them to just "wing it". However, here's how it might work:

1. **Set Parameters**: Provide your teen with the weekly or monthly grocery budget and discuss any dietary or household

requirements (e.g., "We need enough for breakfast, lunch, and dinner for four people, including school lunches").

2. **Offer Resources**: Show them how to make a shopping list, compare prices, or find deals online. Then let them decide which tools they'll use.

3. **Step Back**: Allow them to take full responsibility, including the possibility of mistakes. If they run out of money before meeting all the household needs, resist the urge to rescue them immediately. Instead, use this as an opportunity for problem-solving.

4. **Debrief Together**: At the end of the two weeks or month, sit down and reflect. What went well? What would they do differently next time? Use this conversation to reinforce the lessons learned without judgment.

This will take time. This will take effort. This will take allowing natural mistakes and consequences to occur. You will need to become as comfortable as possible with unfavorable outcomes. When your child was learning to walk, sometimes they fell down. Expect tumbles in this phase from both you and your teen.

Building on Existing Research:

The MBM approach draws on well-established research about the importance of autonomy in adolescence. For example, studies published in the Journal of Adolescence show that teens who are given age-appropriate independence develop stronger self-efficacy and decision-making skills. These findings align with the principle of collaborative identity anchoring, which encourages parents to guide rather than dictate.

How This Looks in Practice:

- **Predetermined Leadership Areas**: Before delegating, identify household responsibilities or decisions that can be handed over entirely to your teen. Examples might include planning family meals, managing their own laundry, or scheduling study times or pick up and drop off times for the household members activities and car sharing or chores, yard work or car upkeep. Anything that is commonly part of a request from them, will be the best items for turning over to them.

- **MBM Innovation**: Unlike other methods that focus on shared tasks, MBM emphasizes full leadership within designated areas. This builds a sense of ownership and reinforces trust. You have not used the method, if you are still participating in completing the delegated task. You can give feedback, input, guidance and oversight. That's it.

- **Facilitation Over Supervision**: Once responsibilities are delegated, your role shifts to a facilitator who provides support only when requested. This allows your teen to experience both the rewards and consequences of their choices.

- Example: If your teen takes charge of meal planning and prep, but forgets to check the pantry before making a shopping list, let them navigate the challenge of missing ingredients. If this results in another run to the store and delayed participation in another commitment or activity, do not take over the impacted commitment or activity to soften the consequence. Allow them the space to build resilience.

Connection to MBM:

This practice aligns also with emphasis on experience learning. By giving teens the space to lead and make mistakes, you're reinforcing their problem-solving skills and preparing them for adulthood in a way that's both practical and empowering while still having you close enough at hand, but not hovering.

Building Emotional Fortitude

This isn't just about equipping your teen—it's also about preparing yourself. Teens mirror adult behavior, and your ability to manage stress, adapt to change, and respond with patience sets a powerful example. The emphasis is on building emotional fortitude as a critical aspect of preparing for the journey.

The Role of Emotional Modeling:

Taking into account the research from Harvard's Center on the Developing Child, which highlights the importance of co-regulation (the way adults help children regulate their emotions by modeling calmness and stability), the MBM expands this concept just a bit.

Instead of focusing solely on moment-to-moment interactions, the MBM encourages parents to actively strengthen their emotional capacity through deliberate practices.

Intentional choices. Preplanned activities. I hope the repetition is helping you to begin imagining what this can look like for you.

MBM Practices for Emotional Fortitude:

1. **Self-Reflection**: Take time to evaluate your emotional triggers as the facilitator and trainer (detach from parent just temporarily) and how they might influence your parenting. Understanding your own responses allows you to approach challenges with more clarity.

   - **MBM Innovation**: Use journaling or voice memos to reflect on high-stress parenting moments. This practice not only helps you process emotions but also provides insight into patterns that can be addressed and pre planned for the next go around.

2. **Mindfulness and Emotional Regulation**: Activities like meditation, breathwork, or even daily walks can help you stay grounded during emotionally charged situations.

   - **Inspired by Existing Practices**: Mindfulness-based stress reduction (MBSR),

   - developed by Jon Kabat-Zinn, has been shown to reduce anxiety and improve focus. The MBM adapts this by integrating mindfulness into family routines, encouraging parents to model these practices alongside their teens.

Adolescents are bound to test boundaries and make mistakes—it's a natural part of their development. However, how you respond to these moments can either strengthen or weaken your relationship. Building emotional fortitude as a parent means learning to view mistakes as opportunities for growth rather than as failures. By reframing these situations positively, you help your teen develop problem-solving skills, accountability, and resilience.

Neuro-Linguistic Programming (NLP) techniques into your responses can make this process even more effective. NLP focuses on how language and communication influence thoughts, behaviors, and emotions. By using specific phrasing and reframing techniques, you can shift the conversation from blame to growth, creating an empowering and constructive interaction.

Example: A Missed Household Task

Let's say your teen forgets to complete a household task, like taking out the trash or preparing part of a family meal. Instead of reacting with frustration, you can apply NLP techniques to engage them in a problem-solving conversation.

Reframe the Language

- Instead of saying, "Why didn't you do what you were supposed to?" (which implies blame), try reframing with a more neutral and forward-focused question, such as:

- "What got in the way of completing this task?"

- "How can we make sure this gets done next time?"

- This language avoids assigning fault and shifts the focus to identifying solutions, helping your teen feel less defensive and more open to reflecting on their behavior. **Use Positive Presuppositions**

- NLP teaches the power of positive presuppositions—phrases that assume a successful outcome or a solution is possible. For example:

- "I know you're capable of handling this. What do you think would work better next time?"

- "Since you've done this before, what do you think happened this time?"

- These statements communicate confidence in your teen's ability to resolve the issue, reinforcing their self-efficacy and encouraging them to think critically about their actions.

- Anchor the Conversation in Strengths

- In NLP, anchoring involves linking positive emotions or strengths to specific situations. During the conversation, remind your teen of times when they successfully completed a task. For example:

- "Last week, you handled this so well and even went beyond what was needed. What do you think helped you stay on track then?"

- This technique draws attention to their past successes, helping them associate problem-solving with their existing strengths.

- Use Visual or Sensory Language

- NLP emphasizes the importance of connecting with a person's preferred communication style—visual, auditory, or kinesthetic. Tailor your phrasing to match how your teen processes information:

- **Visual**: "Can you picture what the outcome would look like if we handled this differently next time?"

- **Auditory**: "What sounds like a good way to approach this in the future?"

- **Kinesthetic**: "How did it feel when you realized the task wasn't done? How could we create a plan that feels more manageable?"

- Set a Forward-Focused Goal

- NLP often emphasizes the importance of forward momentum. Conclude the conversation with an actionable plan that feels achievable. For example:

- "Let's agree that for the next week, we'll both check in once a day to make sure everything is on track. How does that sound?"

- By framing the resolution as a collaborative effort, you reinforce teamwork and shared accountability, which are key principles of the MBM.

Connection to MBM

This approach ties directly to the MBM's emphasis on collaborative identity anchoring. By responding to mistakes with NLP-informed techniques, you're modeling emotional regulation and constructive communication while empowering your teen to takeresponsibility for their actions. Each interaction reinforces the idea that mistakes aren't failures—they're stepping stones to growth and understanding.

- By combining NLP strategies with the MBM framework, you create a parenting approach that is empathetic, forward-focused, and deeply aligned with your teen's developmental needs.

These practices also align with the core component of managing your emotions effectively by creating an environment where you and your teen feels safe to express themselves, learn from their mistakes, and grow.

Belonging and Identity Begin at Home

One of the most significant influences on a teen's sense of identity is their family. Research from **Dr. Brené Brown** and the work of **Stedman Graham** underscores the importance of belonging, showing that children who feel connected to their families, identify values, and are self aware are better equipped to navigate external pressures and are able to pursue/reciprocate and form healthy relationships.

Building on this research, MBM focuses on helping teens see their family as both a source of support and a space where they can explore their individuality. This is achieved by balancing the need for connection with the freedom to question, challenge, and redefine family norms.

MBM Practices for Fostering Belonging:

- **Family Rituals**: Establish weekly check-ins, shared meals, or joint projects that

- reinforce connection while giving teens space to voice their thoughts and opinions.

- **Shared Leadership**: Allow your teen to take the lead on family decisions occasionally, such as planning a weekend activity or organizing a family event.

- **Open Dialogue**: Create a culture of honest communication where disagreements are seen as opportunities for growth rather than threats to harmony.

Here are four open-ended questions that integrate MBM's Socratic influence, designed to encourage critical thinking and reinforce the value of family as a foundational group for identity development:

Reflecting on Choices:

- "When you think about how you handled that situation, what stands out to you as something you're proud of, and what might you approach differently next time?" **Exploring Family Dynamics**:

- "How do you think our family's way of doing things helps us stay connected, and are there any changes you'd suggest to make it even better?"

Understanding Personal Identity Within the Family:

- "What do you think makes you unique in our family, and how do you think your strengths contribute to who we are as a whole?"

Building Empathy and Perspective:

- "When we have a disagreement or different points of view, what do you think is the best way for us to understand each other better?"

Why This Matters

Preparing yourself for the journey of parenting an adolescent is as much about your growth as it is theirs. By reframing parenting as facilitation and building emotional fortitude, you're not only equipping your teen with the tools they need for independence but also modeling the resilience and adaptability they'll carry into adulthood. These foundational principles can be applied to specific challenges and transitions in adolescence.

QUESTIONS TO CONSIDER

End of Chapter Questions for Parents

1. Self-Reflection:

- *"What traditions, stories, or values from your own upbringing have you shared with your child? Are there any you'd like to revisit or adapt for their current challenges?"*

2. Facilitation Assessment:

- *"What household responsibilities or decisions could you hand over to your teen to help them build independence? How would you ensure they feel supported without stepping in unnecessarily?"*

3. Navigating Emotional Growth:

- *"How do you currently respond when your teen makes a mistake? What changes could you make to encourage a growth mindset while maintaining connection and trust?"*

End of Chapter Questions for Teens

1. Family Connection:

- *"What are some family traditions or stories that you feel connected to? Are there any you'd like to learn more about or create with your family?"*

2. Taking Responsibility:

- *"If you could take charge of one area of the household, like budgeting or planning meals, what would it be? How would you approach it, and what support might you need?"*

3.   Emotional Regulation and Growth:

- *"When you make a mistake or things don't go as planned, what helps you reflect and move forward? Are there ways your family could better support you in those moments?"*

CHAPTER

2

PART II

THE CORE COMPONENTS OF MBM

Pre-Taught and Experience Learning

The concept of pre-taught and experience learning focuses on teaching adolescents foundational concepts at home and in the community before they encounter real-world applications. This approach builds on established educational principles, such as those used in Montessori-style learning, where students explore ideas through hands-on, practical experiences. However, MBM takes this further by tailoring lessons to the unique developmental needs of adolescence, emphasizing "macro-concepts" like emotional resilience, ethical decision-making, and time management.

By combining pre-taught lessons and experiences and activities you set up, the method creates a dynamic framework that supports critical thinking, self-awareness, and personal responsibility. These two components work together: pre-taught learning plants the seeds of understanding, while experience learning nurtures them through practice and reflection.

Introducing New Concepts Without Pressure

Building on the Research of Montessori-Style Learning

Montessori education highlights the importance of introducing ideas in a low-pressure environment, where curiosity drives exploration and mastery develops over time. The MBM incorporates this principle but adapts it for adolescents by focusing on broader life skills and social dynamics.

Unique Approach

In MBM, introducing new concepts without pressure emphasizes creating awareness rather than immediate mastery. Adolescents are presented with "macro-concepts"—big-picture ideas relevant to their development, such as understanding the long-term consequences of social media use, navigating peer relationships, or managing their time effectively. These lessons are intentionally framed as opportunities for discovery rather than tests of competence.

For example, instead of expecting a teen to immediately perfect time management, MBM encourages parents to share a story about a time they struggled with deadlines and what they learned. This storytelling approach reduces pressure by normalizing mistakes and highlighting growth.

Practical Tips for Parents:

- Share personal or family stories that introduce key ideas (e.g., a grandparent's lesson on perseverance).

- Use analogies or parables to make abstract concepts more relatable (e.g., comparing emotional resilience to building muscle through exercise).

- Avoid rigid timelines for understanding; allow teens to revisit concepts as they gain new experiences.

Practical Examples for Daily Life

Existing Practices

Traditional experience learning often involves structured tasks like science experiments or classroom simulations. While these methods are effective, they may not always connect directly to the realities of adolescence.

MBM's Innovative Approach

The MBM bridges this gap by grounding learning through experiences in real-life scenarios that adolescents encounter daily. These activities are designed to simulate adult responsibilities while allowing teens to practice decision-making, problem-solving, and

accountability in a safe, supportive environment. Some families prefer to enroll and pay for extracurricular activities like sports, martial arts or music. While extracurriculars provide structured skill-building and external validation, MBM's experience learning activities focus on real-world application, emotional growth, and personal accountability.

Experience learning activities differ in several key ways:

1. **Encourages Autonomy**

- Unlike extracurriculars, where the curriculum is determined by instructors, MBM activities give teens more control over their learning process. For example, managing a household grocery budget or planning a family event requires them to make decisions, solve problems, and adapt without a predetermined script.

- This autonomy helps teens build confidence in their ability to navigate complex, real-world scenarios independently.

2. **Develops Emotional Resilience**

- MBM activities often involve managing natural consequences, such as the disappointment of burnt cookies or the challenge of working within a budget. These experiences teach teens to manage emotions like frustration, disappointment, or anxiety, building resilience and emotional intelligence.

- In contrast, extracurriculars may shield teens from these real-life stakes, focusing instead on perfecting a specific skill in a controlled setting where mindset and response isn't typically addressed in the environment.

3. **Strengthens Family and Community Bonds**

- Many MBM activities are rooted in family or community contexts, such as shared storytelling sessions or collaborative problem-solving. This approach reinforces the idea that growth and learning are interconnected with relationships, helping teens feel more connected to their families and communities.

- Extracurriculars, while fostering peer connections, often operate outside the family dynamic, potentially limiting opportunities for strengthening family bonds.

Examples:

1. **Community Initiative Project**

- **Scenario**: The teen is tasked with organizing a small event, such as a family game night or a neighborhood cleanup.

- **Goal**: Teach planning, collaboration, and follow-through.

- **Facilitator Role**: Offer guidance when asked but let them lead the process, even if mistakes occur.

2. **Household Budget Management**

- **Scenario**: The teen manages the grocery budget for two weeks, deciding what to buy and tracking expenses.

- **Goal**: Teach financial literacy, prioritization, and the consequences of overspending.

- **Facilitator Role**: Debrief afterward to reflect on what worked and what could be improved.

3. **Story Sharing Sessions**

- **Scenario**: Family members share stories about moral dilemmas they've faced, discussing the outcomes and lessons learned.

- **Goal**: Build ethical decision-making and connect personal beliefs to real-life examples.

These examples emphasize MBM's focus on making learning relevant and engaging for adolescents while equipping them with practical skills.

Allowing Natural Consequences to Teach Responsibility

Building on Developmental Research

Research in adolescent psychology, such as studies published in the **Journal of Adolescence**, highlights the importance of letting teens experience the natural consequences of their actions. This process builds resilience, accountability, and problem-solving skills.

MBM's Unique Perspective

The MBM incorporates this principle but extends it by framing natural consequences as opportunities for guided reflection. Mistakes aren't merely allowed—they're anticipated and treated as integral to the learning process. Parents take on the role of facilitators, helping teens process their experiences and extract meaningful lessons.

Example in Action:

If a teen forgets to set an appointment for a sports physical, leading to a second request from the school or potential drop off of the roster:

- **Traditional Response**: The parent might intervene to prevent the mistake or express frustration afterward.

- **MBM Approach**: The parent allows the mistake to happen and then engages the teen in a reflective conversation:

- *"What do you think happened here?"*

- *"How could we make sure this doesn't happen next time?"*

By focusing on solutions rather than blame, this approach reinforces the idea that mistakes are not failures but stepping stones to growth and realigning oneself toward the desired outcome.

Connection to MBM:

This method aligns with MBM's emphasis on self-directed emotional activity and collaborative identity anchoring, as it helps teens develop both practical skills and a deeper understanding of themselves.

Three Advantages of MBM Experience Learning Activities (Beyond Cost Savings)

1. **Broader Life Skill Development**

- MBM activities are directly tied to practical, transferable life skills like time management, financial literacy, and ethical decision-making.

- Example: Managing a household budget teaches financial planning—a skill teens will use for a lifetime—while a piano lesson might not connect as directly to future responsibilities. Paying the piano lesson bill would.

2. **Immediate Real-World Relevance**

- MBM activities immerse teens in real-world challenges, making learning relevant

- and immediate. Teens see the direct consequences of their choices, which enhances understanding and retention.

- Example: Cooking a family meal requires them to plan, execute, and adjust in real time, whereas extracurriculars often separate skill-building from real-life application.

3. **Flexibility and Personalization**

- MBM activities are adaptable to a teen's unique interests, needs, and family context. Parents can tailor tasks to emphasize specific skills or values they want to instill,

- such as empathy, teamwork, or self-reliance.

- Example: A teen interested in social causes might organize a small community initiative, combining their passion with valuable organizational skills.

Experience learning focuses on hands-on activities where teens engage directly with tasks or challenges to develop skills, self-awareness, and values. Unlike passive forms of learning, this method immerses teens in real-life scenarios, allowing them to reflect on their actions, understand the consequences, and refine their approach.

This approach transforms everyday household and family responsibilities into opportunities for growth, equipping teens with practical tools they'll need in adulthood. For example teaching body care, morals, and values.

Adolescents benefit from understanding how daily habits and personal choices impact their well-being and relationships. Through experience learning, MBM emphasizes hands-on activities that make these lessons tangible and memorable.

Body Care

- **Activity Example**: Develop a weekly meal plan that balances nutrition and personal preferences.

- *Skills Gained*: Health awareness, time management, and decision-making.

- **Activity Example**: Create a morning or evening self-care routine, including hygiene, mindfulness, and physical activity.

- *Skills Gained*: Personal responsibility, habit-building, and self-discipline.

- Morals and Values

- **Activity Example**: Role-play family scenarios where ethical dilemmas arise (e.g., deciding whether to return extra change received at a store).

- *Skills Gained*: Ethical decision-making, empathy, and integrity.

- **Activity Example**: Organize a family volunteering day, such as helping at a local shelter or community cleanup.

- *Skills Gained*: Community awareness, teamwork, and compassion.

- Storytelling, Simulations, and Visual Learning

Storytelling and simulations are core components of MBM's experience learning model, as they engage teens' imaginations and critical thinking skills. These methods connect abstract concepts to relatable, real-world experiences.

Storytelling

- **Activity Example**: Share family stories about overcoming challenges, then discuss how those lessons apply to current situations.

- *Skills Gained*: Perspective-taking, connection to family heritage, and critical thinking.

- Simulations

- **Activity Example**: Assign your teen the role of "household manager" for a day.

- They're responsible for planning meals, delegating chores, and managing schedules.

- *Skills Gained*: Leadership, problem-solving, and organizational skills.

- **Activity Example**: Simulate a financial planning scenario, where teens decide how to allocate a limited budget for a vacation or family outing.

- *Skills Gained*: Financial literacy, prioritization, and collaboration.

- Visual Learning

- **Activity Example**: Create a visual timeline of a project (e.g., hosting a family dinner), tracking tasks, deadlines, and results.

- *Skills Gained*: Planning, time management, and accountability.

- **Activity Example**: Use charts or diagrams to compare the nutritional content of meals, teaching teens to make informed dietary choices.

- *Skills Gained*: Analytical thinking, health awareness, and informed decision-making.

Self-awareness is a foundational skill for emotional intelligence and personal growth. MBM helps teens build this skill by encouraging reflection and accountability in their daily actions.

Activity Examples Journal Reflections:

- After completing a household task, teens journal about what went well, what was challenging, and what they learned.

- *Skills Gained*: Self-reflection, adaptability, and problem-solving.

Personal SWOT Analysis:

- Guide teens through a simple analysis of their Strengths, Weaknesses, Opportunities, and Threats related to managing a specific responsibility (e.g., organizing a family event).

- *Skills Gained*: Self-assessment, strategic thinking, and confidence building.

Feedback Sessions:

- After completing a collaborative task, hold a family discussion where everyone gives constructive feedback and celebrates successes.

- *Skills Gained*: Communication, emotional regulation, and growth mindset.

Building on Existing Practices

Many traditional approaches to teaching life skills rely on structured activities or passive instruction, such as chore charts or lectures about responsibilities. MBM builds on these methods by emphasizing real-world application and reflection. By incorporating storytelling, simulations, and visual tools, the method connects learning to teens' immediate experiences, making it more engaging and meaningful.

MBM's Unique Contribution

MBM is distinctive in its integration of emotional growth and self-awareness into practical activities. The focus isn't just on completing tasks but on understanding how those tasks relate to personal values, family dynamics, and future responsibilities. For example, managing a budget isn't just about math—it's about ethical decision-making, prioritizing needs over wants, and understanding the ripple effects of one's choices.

CHAPTER

3

ACTIVITIES BASED ON AGE GROUP

---

1. **Budgeting and Finances**

   - **Early Adolescence (11–13):**

   - **Activity**: Start with small, manageable tasks like budgeting for a single meal or snack purchase. Provide them with a set amount of money and a list of options, allowing them to make decisions and track spending.

   - *Skills Gained*: Basic math, prioritization, and value assessment.

   - *Facilitator Role*: Offer gentle guidance to ensure they grasp the basic concepts.

   - **Middle Adolescence (14–16):**

   - **Activity**: Task your teen with planning a weekly grocery budget for the household, including comparing prices and making trade-offs between brands or items.

- *Skills Gained*: Financial literacy, planning, and resource management.

- *Facilitator Role*: Discuss their choices afterward, focusing on their decision-making process.

- **Late Adolescence (17–19):**

- **Activity**: Assign your teen the full responsibility of managing a family budget

- category, such as groceries or utilities, for one month. Encourage them to use tools like spreadsheets or budgeting apps.

- *Skills Gained*: Advanced financial planning, negotiation, and accountability.

- *Facilitator Role*: Act as a mentor, offering occasional feedback while giving them autonomy.

2. **Meal Planning and Preparation**

- **Early Adolescence (11–13):**

- **Activity**: Plan and prepare one simple meal (e.g., pasta, salad) under your supervision. Teach basic cooking skills and the importance of balanced nutrition.

- *Skills Gained*: Basic culinary skills, health awareness, and following instructions.

- *Facilitator Role*: Be hands-on, showing them how to safely handle tools and ingredients.

- **Middle Adolescence (14–16):**

- **Activity**: Plan and prepare a full family dinner, including budgeting for ingredients and choosing recipes.

Incorporate a discussion about nutritional value.

- *Skills Gained*: Multi-tasking, creativity, and decision-making.

- *Facilitator Role*: Act as a supportive observer, stepping in only if necessary.

- **Late Adolescence (17–19):**

- **Activity**: Plan a week's worth of meals for the family, shop for ingredients, and cook at least half of the meals independently. Reflect on how well the meals met the family's needs.

- *Skills Gained*: Advanced planning, self-reliance, and feedback processing.

- *Facilitator Role*: Offer constructive feedback and discuss what went well and what could improve.

3. **Household Maintenance**

  - **Early Adolescence (11–13):**

  - **Activity**: Assign responsibility for a specific, smaller task, like keeping the kitchen counters clean or organizing a bookshelf.

  - *Skills Gained*: Basic organizational skills and consistency.

  - *Facilitator Role*: Set clear expectations and celebrate successes to build confidence.

  - **Middle Adolescence (14–16):**

  - **Activity**: Assign a broader responsibility, like maintaining the cleanliness of a shared space (e.g., living room or bathroom) for a week.

  - *Skills Gained*: Accountability, time management, and initiative.

- *Facilitator Role*: Encourage independence but provide reminders as needed.

- **Late Adolescence (17–19):**

- **Activity**: Have them oversee a home maintenance task like organizing a storage space, delegating tasks to family members, and ensuring everything is completed.

- *Skills Gained*: Leadership, project management, and teamwork.

- *Facilitator Role*: Act as a resource if questions arise, but allow them to handle the project fully.

4. **Scheduling and Coordination**

   - **Early Adolescence (11–13):**

   - **Activity**: Plan a family game night or outing, ensuring everyone's preferences are considered.

   - *Skills Gained*: Collaboration, empathy, and basic planning.

   - *Facilitator Role*: Help them brainstorm options and outline the plan.

   - **Middle Adolescence (14–16):**

   - **Activity**: Create a family weekend schedule, balancing commitments like sports, errands, and relaxation time.

   - *Skills Gained*: Time management, prioritization, and adaptability.

   - *Facilitator Role*: Offer feedback on how well the schedule worked.

   - **Late Adolescence (17–19):**

   - **Activity**: Plan and coordinate a multi-day family trip, managing transportation, lodging, and activities.

MAYA BECHI

- *Skills Gained*: Advanced logistical planning, decision-making under constraints, and negotiation.

- *Facilitator Role*: Discuss the plan beforehand and reflect on the experience afterward.

5. **Community Engagement**

   - **Early Adolescence (11–13):**

   - **Activity**: Participate in a community service project, such as helping with a food drive or cleanup.

   - *Skills Gained*: Empathy, teamwork, and civic awareness.

   - *Facilitator Role*: Join them in the activity to model positive engagement.

   - **Middle Adolescence (14–16):**

   - **Activity**: Take the lead in organizing a small service project, such as a neighborhood recycling initiative or a donation drive.

   - *Skills Gained*: Leadership, problem-solving, and collaboration.

   - *Facilitator Role*: Guide them in planning but let them handle execution.

   - **Late Adolescence (17–19):**

   - **Activity**: Develop and execute a long-term community project, like mentoring younger students or leading a sustainability effort.

   - *Skills Gained*: Initiative, project management, and long-term thinking.

   - *Facilitator Role*: Provide mentorship and encourage reflection on the impact of their work.

Why Tailoring Activities Matters

By adjusting tasks to suit the developmental stage of adolescence, MBM ensures that experience learning remains both challenging and achievable. Early adolescents gain foundational skills and confidence, middle adolescents refine their abilities, and late adolescents prepare for full independence. This progression builds a strong sense of self-efficacy, responsibility, and readiness for adulthood.

CHAPTER

COMPLEX ACTIVITIES BASED ON AGE GROUP

Financial Literacy Activities

1. Early Adolescence (11–13)

At this stage, teens are beginning to understand basic money concepts like earning, spending, and saving. Activities should focus on building foundational skills in a low-pressure environment.

- **Allowance Budgeting:**

- **Activity**: Give your teen a small allowance and help them allocate it across spending, saving, and charitable giving.

- **Goal**: Teach the value of money, prioritization, and delayed gratification.

- **Facilitator Role**: Provide guidance, such as setting up jars or envelopes for each category, but allow them to make decisions within the framework.

- **Savings Goal Tracker:**

- **Activity**: Help them set a savings goal for a desired item (e.g., a new video game) and track their progress visually, using charts or apps.

- **Goal**: Reinforce patience, goal-setting, and the relationship between saving and rewards.

- **Facilitator Role**: Encourage them to brainstorm ways to earn additional money, like small chores or tasks for neighbors.

2. **Middle Adolescence (14–16)**

Teens in this stage are ready for more complex financial tasks that involve real-world applications.

- **Event Budgeting:**

- **Activity**: Assign your teen the responsibility of planning a small event, such as a family outing or birthday party, with a set budget.

- **Goal**: Teach cost estimation, trade-offs, and managing unexpected expenses.

- **Facilitator Role**: Act as a resource for questions but let them handle the final decisions. Reflect together on their choices post-event.

- **Mock Investment Game:**

- **Activity**: Introduce basic concepts of investing by using a stock market simulation game. Have them track "investments" over several weeks.

- **Goal**: Teach long-term financial thinking and risk-reward analysis.

- **Facilitator Role**: Help explain investment terms and encourage reflection on how different strategies performed.

3. **Late Adolescence (17–19)**

At this stage, teens are preparing for financial independence and benefit from activities that mirror adult responsibilities.

- **Monthly Budget Management:**

- **Activity**: Provide your teen with a mock monthly "income" and a list of expenses (e.g., rent, utilities, groceries). Have them create and manage a budget.

- **Goal**: Teach real-world budgeting, managing fixed vs. variable costs, and planning for emergencies.

- **Facilitator Role**: Discuss strategies for cutting costs and saving for long-term goals.

- **Personal Finance Planning:**

- **Activity**: Help your teen research and plan for their future financial responsibilities, such as opening a bank account, applying for a credit card, or saving for college.

- **Goal**: Teach financial literacy for independence and the importance of building credit.

- **Facilitator Role**: Guide them through the steps but let them make key decisions about which services or strategies suit their needs.

Emotional Growth Activities

1. **Early Adolescence (11–13)**

Teens in this age group are learning to identify and articulate their emotions. Activities should focus on building emotional vocabulary and practicing basic regulation techniques.

- **Emotion Mapping:**

- **Activity**: Create a chart with common emotions and have your teen identify how they felt during specific moments of the day or week.

- **Goal**: Teach emotional awareness and pattern recognition.

- **Facilitator Role**: Discuss their observations and help them explore why they felt a certain way.

- **Guided Meditation or Breathwork:**

- **Activity**: Practice simple breathing exercises like the "5-5-5" method (inhale for 5 seconds, hold for 5, exhale for 5) together during stressful moments.

- **Goal**: Teach self-regulation and stress reduction.

- **Facilitator Role**: Model the exercises and normalize their use in everyday life.

2. **Middle Adolescence (14–16)**

Teens in this stage are beginning to connect their emotions to actions and relationships. Activities should promote empathy and constructive communication.

- **Family Feedback Sessions:**

- **Activity**: Hold a weekly meeting where each family member shares one positive observation and one constructive piece of feedback.

- **Goal**: Teach communication, empathy, and the ability to receive feedback without defensiveness.

- **Facilitator Role**: Set ground rules for respectful dialogue and model active listening.

- **Emotion-Action Journaling:**

- **Activity**: Encourage your teen to journal about moments of strong emotion, focusing on what triggered it, how they responded, and what they learned.

- **Goal**: Teach self-awareness and the connection between emotions and behavior.

- **Facilitator Role**: Read entries only if they invite you to and discuss their reflections.

3. **Late Adolescence (17–19)**

Older teens benefit from activities that challenge them to take ownership of their emotions and use them constructively.

- **Conflict Resolution Role-Play:**

- **Activity**: Role-play challenging scenarios (e.g., resolving a disagreement with a friend or navigating a workplace conflict) and discuss strategies for resolution.

- **Goal**: Teach advanced emotional regulation, empathy, and negotiation skills.

- **Facilitator Role**: Offer feedback on their approach and suggest alternative strategies if needed.

- **Service as Reflection:**

- **Activity**: Encourage your teen to volunteer in a setting that challenges their emotional resilience, such as a shelter or mentorship program, and reflect on how the experience made them feel and grow.

- **Goal**: Build empathy, perspective, and emotional maturity.

- **Facilitator Role**: Debrief with them after each session to discuss their takeaways.

MAYA BECHI

CHAPTER

COORDINATED ACTIVITIES BASED ON AGE GROUP

1. Family Charity Budget

Age Group Adaptation:

- **Early Adolescence (11–13):** Provide a small family budget for a charitable donation, and let your teen research local organizations to decide where the money should go.

- **Middle Adolescence (14–16):** Include your teen in setting the criteria for the donation (e.g., focusing on environmental causes or community health) and have them present their chosen organization to the family.

- **Late Adolescence (17–19):** Assign them the responsibility of managing the entire process, including budgeting, selecting organizations, and coordinating the donation.

Skills Gained:

- **Financial Literacy:** Budgeting, prioritization, and researching costs.

- **Emotional Growth**: Empathy, community awareness, and decision-making under constraints.

Facilitator Role: Guide discussions about why certain causes matter to them and encourage reflection on the impact of their choice.

2. Family "Business" Simulation

Activity: Create a family "business" project where everyone takes on a specific role (e.g., CEO, accountant, marketer). The goal could be anything from organizing a family yard sale to running a lemonade stand or a bake sale for charity.

Age Group Adaptation:

- **Early Adolescence (11–13)**: Assign simpler roles, such as creating signs or setting up the space.

- **Middle Adolescence (14–16)**: Assign more complex roles like tracking expenses and profits or handling customer interactions.

- **Late Adolescence (17–19)**: Let your teen lead the entire project, including delegating tasks and setting goals.

Skills Gained:

- **Financial Literacy**: Profit tracking, expense management, and cost-benefit analysis.

- **Emotional Growth**: Collaboration, leadership, and managing setbacks.

Facilitator Role: Act as an advisor or "board member," offering support without taking over decision-making.

3. Family Meal Planning Challenge

Activity: Create a family challenge where the goal is to plan, shop for, and cook meals for the week while sticking to a set budget. Include discussions about nutrition and dietary preferences to integrate emotional considerations.

Age Group Adaptation:

- **Early Adolescence (11–13)**: Allow them to choose a few meals and assist with shopping and cooking under supervision.

- **Middle Adolescence (14–16)**: Let them manage the shopping list and budget, with some guidance on nutritional balance.

- **Late Adolescence (17–19)**: Assign full responsibility for the week's meal planning, from budgeting to execution.

Skills Gained:

- **Financial Literacy**: Budgeting, cost comparisons, and efficient shopping.

- **Emotional Growth**: Consideration of others' preferences, patience, and stress management.

Facilitator Role: Provide feedback during the process and reflect on what worked well and what they might adjust next time.

4. *Planning a Family Vacation*

Activity: Task your teen with creating a budget and itinerary for a weekend family trip, considering transportation, accommodations, meals, and activities.

Age Group Adaptation:

- **Early Adolescence (11–13)**: Assist them in researching fun activities and estimating basic costs.

- **Middle Adolescence (14–16)**: Have them create a detailed itinerary with cost estimates for meals and activities.

- **Late Adolescence (17–19)**: Let them manage the entire planning process, including finding deals and presenting their plan to the family.

Skills Gained:

- **Financial Literacy**: Cost analysis, negotiation, and travel budgeting.

- **Emotional Growth**: Balancing family preferences, managing stress, and problem-solving.

Facilitator Role: Debrief after the trip to discuss their experience and what they learned about planning and compromise.

5. Emergency Budget Simulation

Activity: Simulate an unexpected financial challenge (e.g., an appliance breaks, or there's a car repair) and ask your teen to revise a household budget to accommodate the expense.

Age Group Adaptation:

- **Early Adolescence (11–13)**: Walk them through a simplified budget and discuss how to prioritize essentials.

- **Middle Adolescence (14–16)**: Give them a mock budget with realistic expenses and have them reallocate funds.

- **Late Adolescence (17–19)**: Present a complex scenario with multiple variables and have them create a revised budget and contingency plan.

Skills Gained:

- **Financial Literacy**: Emergency planning, resource allocation, and critical thinking.

- **Emotional Growth**: Stress management, adaptability, and responsibility.

Facilitator Role: Guide them through reflecting on how they balanced immediate needs with long-term priorities.

6. Collaborative Home Improvement Project

Activity: Select a home improvement project (e.g., redecorating a room, creating a garden, or organizing storage) and involve your teen in every stage, from budgeting to execution.

Age Group Adaptation:

- **Early Adolescence (11–13)**: Involve them in selecting materials and assisting with smaller tasks.

- **Middle Adolescence (14–16)**: Assign them responsibility for researching costs and organizing supplies.

- **Late Adolescence (17–19)**: Let them lead the project, including setting deadlines, managing the budget, and delegating tasks.

Skills Gained:

- **Financial Literacy**: Budgeting for materials, comparing prices, and evaluating value.

- **Emotional Growth**: Teamwork, leadership, and resilience when faced with unexpected challenges.

Facilitator Role: Support their leadership role by providing encouragement and offering advice when requested.

CHAPTER

6

SPECIFIC INTERESTS ACTIVITIES

Entrepreneurship Focus

1. **Family Business Simulation with a Profit Goal**

   - **Activity**: Have your teen create and run a small business venture, such as selling

   - handmade crafts, baked goods, or digital services. Set a profit goal to give the activity real-world relevance.

   - **Skills Gained**: Budgeting, marketing, customer interaction, and profit analysis.

   - **Facilitator Role**: Act as a "business mentor," providing advice on pricing, branding, or customer outreach.

2. **Shark Tank Pitch Night**

   - **Activity**: Assign your teen the task of developing a business idea and creating a presentation to pitch it to the family as if they're investors. Include details like startup costs, expected profits, and marketing strategies.

- **Skills Gained**: Public speaking, strategic thinking, and financial forecasting.

- **Facilitator Role**: Provide constructive feedback on their pitch and discuss ways to refine their plan.

3. **Project-Based Leadership**

- **Activity**: Encourage your teen to organize a fundraiser or charity drive, handling everything from budgeting to event coordination.

- **Skills Gained**: Leadership, financial planning, and community engagement.

- **Facilitator Role**: Support them in brainstorming and navigating logistical challenges.

Environmentalism Focus

1. **Sustainable Meal Planning Challenge**

- **Activity**: Task your teen with planning a week's worth of meals that emphasize sustainability (e.g., local produce, plant-based ingredients) while sticking to a budget.

- **Skills Gained**: Environmental awareness, budgeting, and health-conscious decision-making.

- **Facilitator Role**: Discuss the environmental impact of their choices and how they balanced sustainability with practicality.

2. **Green Business Simulation**

- **Activity**: Have your teen design and execute an eco-friendly initiative, such as a recycling drive, upcycling project, or community garden.

- **Skills Gained**: Project management, environmental advocacy, and creative problem-solving.

- **Facilitator Role**: Help them identify resources and partnerships to make their project successful.

3. **Energy Audit of the Home**

- **Activity**: Assign your teen to conduct an energy audit of the household, identifying ways to save electricity, water, or gas. Have them create a cost-benefit analysis of implementing changes.

- **Skills Gained**: Analytical thinking, environmental responsibility, and financial literacy.

- **Facilitator Role**: Implement one or more of their suggestions and evaluate the results together.

Artistic Pursuits Focus

1. **Creative Budgeting for an Art Project**

- **Activity**: Give your teen a budget and challenge them to create an art project (e.g., painting, sculpture, or photography series) within those constraints.

- **Skills Gained**: Financial planning, resourcefulness, and creativity.

- **Facilitator Role**: Encourage them to explore cost-effective solutions like repurposing materials.

2. **Artistic Showcase Planning**

- **Activity**: Assign your teen the task of organizing a small showcase for their or their peers' artwork. They must budget for materials, promotion, and display arrangements.

- **Skills Gained**: Event planning, collaboration, and marketing.

- **Facilitator Role**: Help them secure a venue or audience (e.g., the family living room or a school event).

3. **Commissioned Art Simulation**

- **Activity**: Simulate an art commission scenario where they must negotiate with a "client" (a family member) to create a piece within a specified budget and timeline.

- **Skills Gained**: Negotiation, time management, and client relations.

- **Facilitator Role**: Act as the "client" and provide feedback on their process and final product.

General Adaptations for All Interests

For each interest, incorporate **reflective practices** to tie the activity back to MBM's focus on self-awareness and growth. For example:

- **Journaling**: After completing a task, have your teen journal about what they learned, what they enjoyed, and what they found challenging.

- **Family Discussions**: Hold debrief sessions to discuss the broader impact of their project (e.g., "How did this project help you understand your role in the family/community?").

- **Feedback Loops**: Use open-ended questions to encourage critical thinking, such as:

- *"What worked well during this activity, and what would you do differently next time?"*

- *"How did this project connect to your interests and goals?"*

Connection to MBM

These activities align with MBM's principles by:

1. **Building Emotional Resilience**: Teens learn to handle challenges, manage feedback, and adapt their plans.

2. **Fostering Autonomy**: They take ownership of tasks, developing confidence and decision-making skills.

3. **Connecting to Values**: Each activity reinforces the importance of aligning personal interests with broader family or community responsibilities.

CHAPTER

SELF-DIRECTED EMOTIONAL ACTIVITY

Self-directed emotional activity focuses on empowering adolescents to understand, articulate, and regulate their emotional states while fostering family connections. This approach encourages teens to take ownership of their emotional growth, supported by intentional family involvement and tools for self-reflection.

Encouraging Independent Emotional Exploration

Building on the Research of Emotional Intelligence

Research by Daniel Goleman highlights that emotional intelligence (EQ)—the ability to recognize and manage one's emotions—is a key predictor of success in both personal and professional life. While many traditional methods rely on structured group settings like therapy or school-based programs, this framework emphasizes tools and techniques that adolescents can use independently or within their family context.

Innovative Framework: The EMOTION Tip

The "EMOTION Blueprint" is designed to guide teens through a systematic process of emotional self-awareness and growth:

1. **Explore Feelings**: Encourage journaling or voice memos to identify and document emotions as they arise.

2. **Map Out Triggers**: Identify specific situations, environments, or interactions that cause emotional responses, both positive and negative.

3. **Organize Actions**: Develop actionable steps to manage emotions, such as practicing gratitude, setting boundaries, or using calming techniques like breathwork.

4. **Test Solutions**: Experiment with different coping strategies and seek feedback from trusted family members or peers.

5. **Interpret Long-Term Patterns**: Reflect on recurring emotional patterns to understand deeper triggers and responses.

6. **Own Growth**: Regularly assess successes and challenges in emotional regulation, celebrating progress and identifying areas for improvement.

Tools and Resources

To support this process, introduce practical tools such as:

- **Emotion cards**: Cards with prompts for identifying and articulating feelings.

- **Mood Journals**: Structured notebooks with sections for recording emotions, triggers, and coping strategies.

- **Apps**: Technology like mindfulness or mood-tracking apps designed for adolescents to self-monitor their emotional states.

Co-Participating in Emotional Growth Activities

Inspired by Family-Based Emotional Interventions

Studies, such as those from the **Journal of Family Psychology**, emphasize that co-participation in activities strengthens family bonds and emotional regulation. Building on this research, emotional growth activities are designed to include family members while keeping the adolescent's self-discovery at the forefront.

Refined Activities

- **Cultural Recipes**: Cooking specific family or cultural dishes together fosters emotional connection and reinforces a sense of heritage and identity.

- **Family or Cultural Dance**: Engaging in shared physical activities, like salsa or a traditional cultural dance, releases endorphins and builds trust through synchronized movement.

- **Meditation and Breathwork**: Co-practice techniques like guided meditations or the "box breathing" method, which calms the nervous system and models healthy emotional regulation.

- **Replace One Community Activity with Family Time**: Swap an external event (e.g., a sports practice) for a family outing where open discussions about emotional growth are encouraged.

Triggering Positive Hormones and Bonding

The Science Behind Hormonal Responses

Building on research about oxytocin (the "bonding hormone") and dopamine (associated with reward and pleasure), intentional activities can foster emotional resilience and strengthen relationships. Shared moments of vulnerability and success trigger these positive hormones, making emotional regulation a shared journey.

Activities to Trigger Bonding Hormones

1. **Cooking and Eating Together**: Sharing meals prepared collaboratively enhances oxytocin levels, particularly when the meal holds personal or cultural significance.

2. **Heart-Centered Practices**: Use heart intelligence techniques like synchronized breathing while holding a calming or affirming thought, which can reduce stress and promote connection.

3. **Collaborative Gratitude Practice**: End the day with each family member sharing one thing they are grateful for, which enhances dopamine and promotes positive emotional habits.

Practical Steps to Build Emotional Resilience

Inspired by Cognitive Behavioral Techniques

CBT focuses on identifying negative thought patterns and replacing them with healthier ones. Adapted for adolescents, the following steps integrate self-awareness with practical, action-based techniques:

1. **Identify Emotional Triggers**: Work together to pinpoint situations that consistently cause stress or frustration.

2. **Set Emotional Goals**: Encourage teens to identify a specific emotional skill they want to improve (e.g., patience, managing anxiety).

3. **Create a Coping Toolbox**: Develop a personalized "toolbox" of strategies, such as listening to music, taking a walk, or practicing visualization.

4. **Role-Play Scenarios**: Simulate challenging situations, like a disagreement with a friend, and brainstorm responses that align with their emotional goals.

5. **Reflect and Adjust**: Schedule regular check-ins to discuss what strategies worked and what didn't, fostering adaptability and continuous growth.

How This Approach Differs from Existing Practices

While traditional emotional education often relies on structured therapy or teacher-led activities, this approach integrates family involvement, cultural practices, and independent tools. It also focuses on real-world application, where teens actively practice and reflect on their emotional regulation strategies rather than passively learning about them.

Unique Contributions

- The **EMOTION Tip** provides a clear, step-by-step framework for self-directed emotional growth, emphasizing ownership and adaptability.

- Family-focused activities like cultural cooking or dancing enhance bonding while respecting and reinforcing heritage.

- Practical tools like mood journals or apps allow for continuous, independent engagement in emotional growth.

By embedding these practices into daily life, teens not only develop emotional resilience but also learn to integrate their emotions into their broader sense of identity and purpose.

MAYA BECHI

CHAPTER

EMOTION BASED ACTIVITIES

Measuring Emotional Growth Through Culturally Linked Activities

Below is an integration of measurable emotional growth techniques with culturally linked activities tailored for adolescents from minority backgrounds. These examples incorporate the **EMOTION Blueprint** framework and emphasize heritage, identity, and family connections.

1. Culturally Rooted Journaling

Activity: Create a mood journal that includes cultural prompts, encouraging teens to reflect on their emotions in relation to their heritage.

- **Example Prompts:**

- *"What family tradition made you feel connected or proud today?"*

- *"How did learning about a cultural hero or story inspire your emotions?"*

- *"Was there a moment when you felt disconnected from your culture? How did you respond?"*

Measurement:

- Review the journal weekly to track patterns in emotional triggers, resilience, and identity-based reflections.

- Look for improvements in emotional articulation (e.g., transitioning from "I felt bad" to "I felt anxious because I didn't know how to express my opinion").

2. Cooking and Family Storytelling

Activity: Involve teens in cooking culturally significant recipes while sharing stories about their origins and meaning. Encourage them to ask questions and reflect on the emotional connections they feel.

- **Example**: Prepare dishes like gumbo (Creole culture), tamales (Aztec or Mayan culture), or dumplings (Asian culture) while discussing the family's connection to the dish.

- **EMOTION Tip Integration:**

- *Explore*: Encourage the teen to share how they feel while cooking.

- *Map*: Discuss the triggers (e.g., feeling pride, joy, or curiosity) linked to this shared experience.

- *Organize*: Suggest they write or record their reflections on how this activity ties to their identity.

Measurement:

- Observe whether participation leads to greater family engagement and emotional expression during these sessions.

- Track their ability to articulate the connection between the activity and their feelings of belonging or pride.

3. Cultural Dance or Movement Practices

Activity: Engage in a family dance night featuring cultural dances (e.g., salsa, African drumming, Indigenous dances).

- **Example**: Practice basic salsa steps together and talk about its Afro-Caribbean origins or participate in a drumming session while discussing its role in African heritage.

- **Triggering Positive Hormones**: Physical activity releases endorphins, and shared cultural moments build oxytocin, enhancing emotional regulation.

- **Reflection Question**: *"How did moving to this music make you feel connected to your culture or family?"*

Measurement:

- Use pre- and post-activity check-ins to assess changes in mood and energy levels.

- Track their willingness to engage in similar activities over time, noting improvements in emotional openness.

4. *Mood Mapping with Visuals and Symbols*

Activity: Create a mood map using culturally significant symbols to represent emotions.

- **Example**: A Native American teen might use animal symbols (e.g., eagle for freedom, turtle for patience) to map out their feelings. A teen from an Afro-Caribbean background might incorporate colors tied to their cultural identity (e.g., red, green, and gold) to express emotions.

EMOTION Blueprint Integration:

- *Explore*: Use symbols to identify emotions after significant events (e.g., a school presentation or family gathering).

- *Interpret*: Discuss what recurring symbols reveal about their emotional patterns.

Measurement:

- Over time, note whether their ability to identify and express emotions becomes more nuanced.

- Look for increased use of positive symbols when reflecting on their daily experiences.

5. *Community-Based Emotional Growth*

Activity: Replace a non-essential extracurricular with a community-based activity tied to their cultural heritage.

- **Example**: Participate in volunteering at a cultural center, attending a heritage festival, or mentoring younger children within their community.

Reflection Questions:

- "What emotions did you feel while participating in this activity?"

- "How did this experience help you connect with your culture and values?"

Measurement:

- Use the EMOTION Tip steps to reflect on the impact of their participation:

- *Map*: Identify how these activities make them feel connected to their community.

- *Own*: Journal or record voice memos about their personal growth and cultural pride.

- Track growth in empathy and self-confidence, particularly in their ability to articulate how they've contributed to their community.

6. *Collaborative Gratitude Practice*

Activity: End each day with a family gratitude practice linked to cultural values or shared experiences.

- **Example**: In a Latinx family, teens might express gratitude for communal meals and the family's emphasis on togetherness. In an Asian household, gratitude might focus on honoring elders' wisdom or sacrifices.

Practical Steps:

- Each family member shares one thing they are grateful for, connecting it to their heritage when possible.

- Encourage teens to reflect on how gratitude shifts their emotional state.

Measurement:

- Observe whether gratitude practices lead to fewer emotional outbursts or negative self-talk.

- Track the teen's willingness to share deeper reflections over time.

7. *Role-Playing Cultural Scenarios*

Activity: Role-play common emotional challenges in cultural contexts, such as addressing microaggressions, navigating stereotypes, or responding to cultural expectations.

- **Example**: Role-play a scenario where a teen is asked to explain their cultural traditions in class, focusing on how to handle discomfort and educate peers.

EMOTION Tip Integration:

- *Test*: Have them try different strategies (e.g., humor, direct communication) and discuss the outcomes.

- *Own*: Encourage self-reflection on what approach felt most authentic and effective.

Measurement:

- Assess improvements in their confidence and ability to respond to emotionally charged situations with clarity and composure.

CHAPTER

COLLABORATIVE IDENTITY ANCHORING

Collaborative identity anchoring is an intentional approach to supporting adolescents in forming a strong, adaptable sense of self. It reimagines traditional parenting roles as facilitation, where adults act as mentors or coaches, emphasizing mutual learning and shared growth. This method fosters decision-making, conflict resolution, digital resilience, and connections with both online and real-life communities. At its core is the belief that guiding adolescents through identity formation collaboratively allows them to develop confidence, self-awareness, and the ability to navigate complex social dynamics.

Planning Physical Contact and Real-Life Community

Building on the Research of Healthy Relationships

Research on adolescent development, such as studies from the **American Psychological Association**, underscores the importance of positive physical contact and face-to-face interactions in building trust, emotional security, and social skills. Collaborative identity anchoring takes this further by weaving healthy touch and real-life community-building into daily life, helping teens feel grounded in their relationships and connected to their values.

Innovative Practices

1. **Healthy Physical Touch**

   - Physical affection, such as hugs, high-fives, or pats on the back, can reinforce trust and emotional safety.

   - Example: Establishing a family ritual like a hug or handshake when saying goodbye or resolving conflicts to symbolize unity and support.

2. **Face-to-Face Community Activities**

   - Encourage adolescents to engage in shared experiences that foster connection.

   - Example: Organize a weekly family dinner where everyone shares stories from their week or participate in cultural or community events, such as festivals or volunteering opportunities.

Digital Resilience and Healthy Online Interactions

Inspired by Digital Literacy Research

As teens spend more time online, the ability to navigate digital spaces safely and responsibly has become essential. Research by organizations like **Common Sense Media** highlights the importance of teaching digital literacy and fostering resilience in the face of cyberbullying, misinformation, and social comparison. Collaborative identity anchoring integrates these principles into actionable steps that empower teens to build a healthy digital presence.

Innovative Practices

1. **Digital Community Participation**

   - Facilitate conversations about how to engage in positive online interactions, such as joining forums or groups aligned with their interests.

   - Example: If a teen is passionate about gaming, encourage them to participate in communities that promote collaborative play and respectful communication.

2. **Resilience Training Through "What If" Scenarios**

   - Use hypothetical situations to help teens practice responding to online challenges.

   - Example: Ask, *"What would you do if a classmate posted something negative about you online?"* Encourage them to brainstorm solutions, like blocking the user, seeking support, or addressing the issue calmly.

3. **Digital Boundaries and Self-Reflection**

   - Encourage teens to set limits on screen time and reflect on how online interactions make them feel.

   - Example: Use prompts like, *"Which online interactions made you feel good today? Which didn't?"* to foster self-awareness.

Decision-Making and Conflict Resolution Skills

Building on Collaborative Problem-Solving Models

Frameworks like **Collaborative and Proactive Solutions (CPS)** emphasize engaging children and teens in solving problems collaboratively rather than imposing solutions.

Collaborative identity anchoring adapts this by focusing on shared decision-making and conflict resolution, helping teens develop critical thinking and communication skills.

Innovative Practices

1. **Group Decision-Making Exercises**

- Include teens in family decisions, such as planning a vacation or organizing schedules.

- Example: Present options for a family trip and let the teen research and propose itineraries, balancing the needs and preferences of the group.

2. **Conflict Resolution Role-Plays**

- Practice resolving common conflicts using role-playing.

- Example: Simulate a scenario where siblings argue over shared responsibilities, guiding them to negotiate a solution.

3. **Celebrating Effort Over Outcomes**

- When conflicts arise, emphasize the process of finding solutions rather than focusing solely on results.

- Example: After a disagreement is resolved, reflect as a family on what worked well in the resolution process.

Framework: The ANCHOR Plan

The ANCHOR plan provides a structured yet flexible framework to guide parents in collaborative identity anchoring:

1. **Ask Open-Ended Questions**

- Encourage reflection by asking questions like, *"What does success mean to you?"* or

- *"How do you want to contribute to the family or community?"*

2. **Navigate Challenges Together**

- Instead of providing direct solutions, guide them in evaluating their options.

- Example: After a poor decision, ask, *"What would you do*

differently next time?"

3. Co-Create Rituals

- Establish family or personal traditions that celebrate individuality and shared values.

- Example: Create a family journal where everyone writes about a weekly accomplishment or challenge.

4. Hold Space for Exploration

- Allow teens to experiment with new identities, hobbies, or social groups without judgment.

- Example: If a teen wants to explore a new style or interest, engage them in discussions about what it means to them and how it aligns with their values.

5. Offer Balanced Feedback

- Focus feedback on effort and growth rather than outcomes.

- Example: *"I noticed how much thought you put into solving that problem. What did you learn from it?"*

6. Reaffirm Autonomy

- Validate their choices and reflections, even if they differ from your expectations.

- Example: *"It's great that you made a decision based on what felt right for you. How does it feel to take ownership of that choice?"*

Specific Scenarios

Identity Portfolio

- **Activity**: Help your teen curate an "identity portfolio," where they document their interests, goals, and personal narratives through writing, photos, or art.

- *Goal*: Encourage self-reflection and provide a tangible way to track personal growth.

Peer Workshops or Group Discussions

- **Activity**: Facilitate group discussions or workshops where teens collaborate on solving a problem or planning a project.

- *Goal*: Build teamwork, communication, and critical thinking skills.

- *Example*: Organize a project where teens brainstorm ways to improve their community, like starting a recycling initiative.

The ANCHOR Plan

Below are detailed templates for using the ANCHOR plan to address common family challenges, including creative solutions for polarizing topics such as **social media use** and **differing political or social beliefs**. These templates guide parents and teens through collaborative identity anchoring while fostering mutual understanding and growth.

Template 1: Addressing Social Media Use

Challenge: Balancing teens' desire for online connection with parents' concerns about screen time, privacy, and mental health.

1. **Ask Open-Ended Questions**

   - *"What do you enjoy most about social media?"*

   - *"How do you think your online presence reflects who you are?"*

2. **Navigate Challenges Together**

   - *Present a realistic scenario: "Imagine a friend posts something about you online that you didn't want shared. How would you handle it?"*

   - Discuss possible actions and their consequences, such as addressing the friend, reporting the post, or seeking support.

3. **Co-Create Rituals**

- Establish family "digital detox" times, such as device-free meals or a weekly offline activity. Make these moments feel like opportunities for connection rather than restrictions.

- Example: "Board Game Night" replaces an evening of scrolling, with teens choosing the game to empower their involvement.

4. **Hold Space for Exploration**

- Encourage your teen to create content that reflects their passions, such as art, music, or causes they care about.

- *"Would you like to share your creative side online in a way that inspires others? How might you do that?"*

5. **Offer Balanced Feedback**

- Acknowledge efforts to use social media positively: *"I noticed you shared that post about environmental awareness. That was thoughtful and showed your values."*

6. **Reaffirm Autonomy**

- Validate their decisions: *"You've taken steps to manage your time online and stay safe. How has that felt for you?"*

Outcome: The teen feels heard and empowered to make mindful choices about social media use while strengthening family connections through collaborative rituals.

Template 2: Navigating Differing Political or Social Beliefs

Challenge: Teens begin to form opinions that diverge from family values, leading to potential conflicts or misunderstandings.

1. **Ask Open-Ended Questions**

- *"What sparked your interest in this topic?"*

- *"How do you feel your beliefs align with your values?"*

2. Navigate Challenges Together

- Present a "what if" scenario: *"Imagine a heated debate with someone who disagrees with your view. How would you approach that conversation?"*

- Explore strategies like active listening, sharing personal perspectives calmly, or finding common ground.

3. Co-Create Rituals

- Host regular "debate nights" where family members discuss a topic respectfully, with each person presenting their perspective and asking questions.

- Example: Rotate topics such as climate change, voting, or school policies, ensuring the teen's topics are prioritized to encourage engagement.

4. Hold Space for Exploration

- Encourage teens to research their beliefs independently while maintaining open dialogue.

- *"What sources do you trust most on this topic, and why?"*

5. Offer Balanced Feedback

- Focus on their thought process rather than agreement: *"I appreciate the way you explained your perspective. It shows you've thought deeply about this."*

6. Reaffirm Autonomy

- Validate their growing independence: *"I respect that you're forming your own opinions. It's okay for us to see things differently as long as we keep listening to each other."*

Outcome: The teen gains confidence in their ability to articulate and refine their views while learning to engage respectfully with differing perspectives.

Template 3: Managing Household Responsibilities

Challenge: A teen resists participating in household tasks, leading to friction over shared responsibilities.

1. **Ask Open-Ended Questions**

   - *"What household task would you feel most comfortable taking responsibility for?"*

   - *"What do you think a fair division of responsibilities looks like in a family?"*

2. **Navigate Challenges Together**

   - Use a practical scenario: *"If the trash isn't taken out and it overflows, what's the best way to prevent that from happening again?"*

   - Discuss how shared responsibilities impact the family dynamic.

3. **Co-Create Rituals**

   - Introduce a "household swap" day where family members exchange tasks to appreciate each other's roles and responsibilities.

Example: The teen handles cooking for the day while a parent takes on a chore typically managed by the teen.

1. **Hold Space for Exploration**

   - Allow teens to experiment with managing a specific area of the household, such as meal planning or laundry, for a week.

   - *"What would it feel like to be in charge of this task for a week? What would you need to succeed?"*

2. **Offer Balanced Feedback**

   - Highlight effort and initiative: *"I saw how much thought you put into planning dinner. That was impressive!"*

3. **Reaffirm Autonomy**

- Empower them with decision-making authority: *"It's up to you how to approach this task. I trust you to figure out what works best."*

Outcome: The teen learns the value of shared responsibilities while gaining independence and confidence in managing household tasks.

Template 4: Exploring Identity Through Hobbies and Interests

Challenge: A teen struggles to balance new hobbies with existing responsibilities or feels uncertain about trying something unfamiliar.

1. **Ask Open-Ended Questions**

- *"What drew you to this new hobby?"*

- *"How do you think this interest connects to your goals or values?"*

2. **Navigate Challenges Together**

- Pose a scenario: *"What would you do if your hobby conflicted with a family responsibility, like a chore or event?"*

- Brainstorm strategies for balancing priorities.

3. **Co-Create Rituals**

- Celebrate the hobby by designating time for the family to support or participate.

- Example: If the teen loves painting, hold a family art night where everyone creates something.

4. **Hold Space for Exploration**

- Encourage trying out the hobby without fear of judgment or pressure to excel.

- *"What do you enjoy most about this activity? Is there a part you'd like to explore further?"*

5. **Offer Balanced Feedback**

- Focus on their passion and growth: *"You've really put effort into learning this skill. It's great to see how much you're enjoying it."*

6. **Reaffirm Autonomy**

- Let them set their own goals: *"You decide how much time to dedicate to this. What feels manageable with everything else going on?"*

Outcome: The teen feels supported in pursuing their interests while learning to balance responsibilities and personal growth.

MAYA BECHI

CHAPTER

10

PART III

PRACTICAL APPLICATIONS

Practical Applications: Reclaiming Time and Energy

Reclaiming Time

Reclaiming time begins with evaluating your family's schedule to identify commitments that may not serve your long-term priorities. A significant time drain for many families is extracurricular activities or sports that demand full-day commitments on weekends. While these activities can provide value, they often come at the expense of family connection, rest, and the opportunity to manage household responsibilities collaboratively.

Evaluating Long-Term Benefits vs. Family Focus

- If a sport or extracurricular involves traveling and attending games or meets that consume an entire day or weekend, consider its impact on your family's energy and cohesion. Does this activity align with your teen's passions and long-term goals? Or is it more of a routine or obligation?

- For instance, pausing an activity like competitive swimming for a season could reclaim several Saturdays and create space for family-centered activities, like planning and cooking meals together or tackling home projects collaboratively.

How Time Reclamation Benefits Parents and Teens

- By skipping such time-intensive commitments, parents reduce their stress levels and gain energy to engage more meaningfully with their children. Instead of rushing through errands or catching up on chores late at night, parents can delegate tasks, allowing teens to step into roles that promote responsibility and collaboration.

- Example: With the regained time from skipping a weekend-long event, a teen can manage grocery shopping or meal prep while parents focus on other family priorities. This redistribution of tasks lightens the load on parents and helps teens build life skills.

Reflection Question: What current activities could your family adjust or pause to reclaim time for connection and collaborative responsibilities?

Reclaiming Energy

Energy is often depleted by overpacked schedules, including managing household responsibilities while supporting demanding extracurricular commitments. Reclaiming energy involves not just redistributing tasks but also creating a family rhythm that prioritizes restoration and presence.

The Energy Cost of Overcommitment

Weekend-long sports tournaments or full-day activities can leave parents juggling late-night household duties or sacrificing personal time. This dynamic creates stress and reduces the energy available for meaningful family interactions.

Swapping Activities for Restorative Family Time

By stepping back from an activity that consumes entire weekends, families can use that time to engage in tasks that reduce stress and strengthen connections:

- **Household Collaboration**: Instead of spending the day at a soccer game, the family might work together on deep-cleaning the home, organizing a cluttered area, or tackling a long-neglected DIY project.

- **Restorative Activities**: The regained time can be used for slow, restorative activities like a leisurely family breakfast, hiking together, or simply staying home to recharge.

Example

Imagine a family that regularly spends 12 hours every Saturday at a volleyball tournament. By pausing this activity for one season, the family could instead dedicate their Saturdays to shared responsibilities like rotating meal prep or planning family game nights. This adjustment not only fosters teamwork but also provides everyone with the downtime needed to recharge for the week ahead.

Reducing Parental Stress Through Delegation

When families shift their focus from extracurriculars to collaborative responsibilities, parents benefit from a lighter workload. Teens who step into roles like managing weekly laundry or taking charge of meal planning contribute to a smoother household dynamic, freeing parents to focus on personal restoration or family bonding.

Reflection Question: How would shifting from time-intensive activities to collaborative household tasks impact your family's energy and connections?

Conclusion

Reclaiming time and energy by evaluating extracurricular commitments and redistributing household responsibilities offers long-term benefits for both parents and teens. By weighing the value of weekend-consuming activities against the benefits of family presence and teamwork, families can create a more balanced and restorative dynamic. These adjustments empower teens with life skills, reduce parental stress, and foster deeper family connections.

The Decision-Making Framework: E.A.S.E. (Evaluate, Align, Streamline, Enrich)

Step 1: Evaluate the Activity

This step helps assess whether the activity aligns with your family's priorities and your teen's overall well-being.

Questions to Ask:

1. *Does this activity support academic growth, personal identity development, or self-awareness?*

2. *Is this activity something my teen is genuinely passionate about or just feels obligated to do?*

3. *How much time does this activity consume weekly (including travel and prep)? Does this time outweigh its benefits?*

4. *What impact does this activity have on my teen's sleep, downtime, or overall mental health?*

Action:

Create a simple scoring system (e.g., 1–5) to rate the activity's alignment with each question. Activities scoring low may be candidates for adjustment or removal.

Step 2: Align with Family Priorities

After evaluating the activity, consider whether it fits within your family's core values of academics, self-awareness, and bonding.

Family-Centered Questions:

1. *Does this activity offer opportunities for family involvement or shared experiences?*

- Example: Attending games together can foster bonding, but if this isn't feasible, its family value might diminish.

2. *Does this activity contribute to my teen's sense of identity or personal growth?*

- Example: A cultural dance class might resonate deeply with their heritage, reinforcing identity anchoring.

Action:

If an activity aligns with a priority but presents challenges (e.g., long hours), explore ways to adjust. For example, can they reduce practice days or limit participation to local events?

Step 3: Streamline Commitments

Over-scheduling is a common cause of stress. This step focuses on reducing the burden of time-intensive activities.

Streamlining Strategies:

1. **Pause for Reflection**: Consider pausing one activity for a season to reassess its value and impact.

- Example: Skipping a semester of travel soccer might allow your teen to focus on academics and enjoy more downtime.

2. **Limit Overlap**: If multiple activities run simultaneously, prioritize the one with the greatest long-term benefits and align the rest with future availability.

3. **Combine Activities**: Look for opportunities to integrate priorities.

- Example: If your teen loves art but is over-scheduled, consider replacing a sports activity with an art class that doubles as a family hobby (e.g., attending painting workshops together).

Step 4: Enrich with Alternatives

Replacing time-intensive activities with meaningful alternatives ensures your teen continues to grow while regaining balance.

Enrichment Options:

1. **Family Bonding Activities**: Use reclaimed time for collaborative cooking, family hikes, or storytelling evenings.

2. **Identity Anchoring**: Encourage self-awareness through journaling, mood mapping, or a creative project that reflects their interests.

3. **Academics and Rest**: Dedicate free time to quiet study sessions, sleep hygiene improvements, or mindfulness practices that reduce stress and improve focus.

Example of Swap:

Instead of a weekend swim meet, plan a Saturday morning breakfast where teens lead discussions about their week. Follow it with a collaborative family activity, such as reorganizing a shared space or planning meals for the week.

Assessing Long-Term Impact

Revisit this framework periodically to assess its effectiveness. Questions to reflect on after a few months include:

1. *How has the change in commitments affected our family dynamics, downtime, and stress levels?*

2. *Has my teen shown improved academic focus, sleep quality, or emotional resilience?*

3. *Are the activities we kept or added fostering deeper connections and self-awareness?*

Reflection Questions

1. *How does this activity contribute to your teen's growth versus the stress it adds to the family dynamic?*

2. *What alternatives could provide similar benefits without the same time or*

energy demands?

3. *How can you involve your teen in evaluating and deciding which activities to keep, adjust, or let go?*

MAYA BECHI

CHAPTER

SCORING SHEETS

E.A.S.E. Scoring Worksheet

Purpose: Evaluate extracurricular activities so you can decide if they are in alignment with your family's priorities and what their impact on time and energy has become.

1.E.A.S.E. Scoring Worksheet

Purpose: Evaluate extracurricular activities to determine their alignment with your family's priorities and their impact on time and energy.

| Activity Name: _____ | Date _____ |

Category	Question	Score (1–5)	Comment
Evaluate	Does this activity support academic growth, personal identity, or self-awareness?		
	Does my teen genuinely enjoy this activity, or do they feel obligated to participate?		
	How much time does this activity consume weekly (including travel and prep)?		
	What impact does this activity have on my teen's sleep, downtime, or mental health?		
Align	Does this activity offer opportunities for family involvement or bonding?		
	Does this activity contribute to my teen's sense of identity or long-term goals?		
Streamline	Can this activity be paused, reduced, or replaced with an alternative that better supports our family's priorities?		
Enrich	Could time spent on this activity be redirected to something restorative, like family bonding or individual growth?		

Scoring Key:

- 1: Strongly Disagree
- 3: Neutral
- 5: Strongly Agree

Total Score: _____

Decision: Keep / Adjust / Pause

1. Weekly Activity Tracker

2. Weekly Activity Tracker

Purpose: Monitor weekly commitments and ensure alignment with family priorities

| Week of: _____ |

Day	Activity/Commitment	Time Spent (hrs)	Family Involvement (Y/N)	Energy Impact (Low/Medium/High)	Note
Monday					
Tuesday					
Wednesday					
Thursday					
Friday					
Saturday					
Sunday					

Reflection:

- Which activities align most with our family priorities?
- Which commitments caused the most stress or required significant time?
- What changes can we make for next week?

Purpose: Monitor weekly commitments and ensure alignment with family priorities.

2. Reflection Worksheet

3. Reflection Worksheet

Purpose: Evaluate changes over time to assess the impact of adjustments on your family's time, energy, and connections.

| Reflection Date: _____ |

Category	Question	Your Reflections
Reclaiming Time	How has our schedule changed since making adjustments to extracurricular activities?	
	What new family activities or routines have we added to replace paused commitments?	
Reclaiming Energy	How has our family's overall energy level improved? Have we reduced stress or burnout?	
	Have collaborative household responsibilities eased the burden on parents and empowered teens?	
Family Dynamics	Have these changes strengthened our family bond?	
	How have these adjustments impacted communication and teamwork in our family?	
Teen Development	Is my teen showing improved self-awareness, sleep quality, or mental health?	
	Have they demonstrated greater responsibility or engagement in family life?	

Action Plan for Next Month:

- **Keep Doing**: What worked well and should continue?
- **Adjust**: What could be modified for better results?
- **Eliminate**: What isn't working and should be reconsidered?

Purpose: Evaluate changes over time to assess the impact of adjustments on your family's time, energy, and connections.

How to Use These Tools

1. **Initial Assessment**: Use the **Scoring Worksheet** to evaluate all current extracurricular activities and identify potential adjustments.

2. **Weekly Monitoring**: Fill out the **Weekly Activity Tracker** to see how time is allocated and identify stressors or imbalances.

3. **Ongoing Reflection**: Complete the **Reflection Worksheet** monthly to assess progress and make iterative changes.

MAYA BECHI

CHAPTER

12

TAILORING MBM TO YOUR HOME DYNAMICS

The MBMethod is flexible and adaptable, designed to meet the unique needs of various home dynamics. Whether your household includes two lead adults, extended family, or is led by a single parent, the MBM framework provides strategies to navigate these configurations effectively. This section explores how to tailor MBM principles to specific family structures and addresses common challenges like resistance from adolescents, consistency, and maintaining patience.

Two-Lead Adult Homes

Key Strengths: Shared responsibilities, aligned goals, and the opportunity to model teamwork for adolescents.

Strategies:

1. **Align on Core Values**

   - Establish a unified vision for family priorities, such as shared values around academics, family bonding, and identity development.

- Example: Hold weekly discussions to ensure both adults are on the same page about household rules and adolescent expectations.

2. **Divide and Conquer**

- Share facilitation roles based on individual strengths. One adult might excel at mentoring academic growth, while the other focuses on emotional support.

- Example: Alternate leading family activities, like one partner handling a storytelling night and the other guiding a collaborative cooking session.

3. **Model Conflict Resolution**

- Show adolescents how healthy disagreements are resolved through communication and compromise.

- Example: Let teens witness respectful discussions between adults about household decisions to reinforce collaborative problem-solving.

Extended Family or Blended Communities

Key Strengths: Broader support network, diverse perspectives, and opportunities to connect with heritage and culture.

Strategies:

1. **Celebrate Diversity in Roles**

- Assign responsibilities to family members based on their strengths, such as a grandparent sharing cultural stories or a sibling mentoring younger children.

- Example: Create a "family council" where everyone contributes ideas for solving a household issue.

2. **Establish Shared Rituals**

- Develop rituals that involve all family members, such as

monthly cultural celebrations or shared projects.

- Example: Plan a family tree activity where teens interview relatives and document their heritage, fostering identity anchoring.

3. **Set Clear Boundaries**

- In blended families, clarify roles and expectations to avoid confusion or conflict.

- Example: Define who manages specific household responsibilities or decisions to create consistency.

Single Parent or Independent Youth Homes

1. **Key Strengths: Opportunity to build resilience, independence, and close parent-teen collaboration.**

2. **Maximize Efficiency**

- Use MBM tools like the E.A.S.E. tracker to streamline activities and prioritize family bonding.

- Example: Skip a non-essential extracurricular and replace it with a collaborative home improvement project that teaches responsibility.

3. **Empower Teens with Ownership**

- Involve adolescents in decision-making to foster their autonomy and reduce the burden on the parent.

- Example: Allow your teen to manage weekly meal planning or grocery shopping with a set budget.

4. **Lean on Community Support**

- Build a network of trusted friends, neighbors, or mentors to provide additional guidance and mentorship for teens.

- Example: Arrange a monthly "skills exchange" where your teen learns practical skills from a community member, like car maintenance or sewing.

Dealing with Resistance

Navigating Pushback from Adolescents

Resistance is a normal part of adolescence, as teens assert their independence and test boundaries. Viewing pushback as an opportunity for dialogue can shift the dynamic from conflict to collaboration.

Strategies:

1. **Listen Before Reacting**

   - Ask open-ended questions to understand their perspective.

   - Example: *"What about this new responsibility feels overwhelming to you?"*

2. **Reframe Tasks as Opportunities**

   - Present responsibilities as ways for them to gain independence or life skills.

   - Example: *"Managing the grocery budget will give you the confidence to handle money when you're on your own."*

3. **Provide Options**

   - Offer choices to give them a sense of control.

   - Example: *"Would you prefer to handle laundry or meal prep this week?"*

Staying Consistent Despite Challenges

Consistency is crucial for reinforcing expectations and creating stability, even when faced with resistance or competing demands.

Strategies:

1. **Set Clear Expectations**

   - Define household routines and stick to them, even during busy times.

- Example: Maintain a nightly device-free dinner policy, regardless of school or work schedules.

2. **Celebrate Small Wins**

   - Recognize and reward progress to keep teens motivated.

   - Example: Praise their effort after they complete a new task, like *"I appreciate how you took charge of this responsibility—it really made a difference."*

3. **Adapt When Needed**

   - Flexibility is part of consistency. Adjust expectations temporarily during high-stress periods, then return to regular routines.

   - Example: Allow a break from chores during exam week but reinforce the expectation afterward.

The Role of Patience and Persistence

Patience and persistence are essential for navigating resistance and maintaining long-term consistency. Building habits and fostering growth take time, and setbacks are part of the process.

Strategies:

1. **Focus on the Bigger Picture**

   - Remind yourself and your teen of the long-term benefits of the MBM approach, such as improved life skills, family bonding, and self-awareness.

   - Example: Share a personal story about how persistence helped you overcome a challenge.

2. **Practice Self-Care**

   - Parents also need downtime to recharge and remain patient.

   - Example: Set aside 15 minutes daily for mindfulness or a calming activity that helps you reset.

3. Model Resilience

- Show your teen how to handle setbacks with grace, reinforcing the value of persistence.

- Example: If a family ritual doesn't go as planned, reflect together on what can improve next time without blame.

Reflection Questions

1. **For Two-Lead Adult Homes**: How can both adults collaborate effectively to present a united approach?

2. **For Blended or Extended Families**: What rituals or practices can strengthen connections across multiple generations or perspectives?

3. **For Single Parent Homes**: What responsibilities can be shared or delegated to reduce stress while building your teen's independence?

4. Additional Tools for Tailoring MBM to Family Dynamics

Below are specific tools designed to help families implement the Maya Bechi Method effectively across various dynamics. These include **conversation prompts**, **shared ritual ideas**, and a **task-sharing guide** to foster collaboration and connection.

1. Conversation Prompts for Family Dynamics

2. **For Two-Lead Adult Homes**

3. *"What shared values do we want to model for our teens, and how can we reinforce those daily?"*

4. *"How can we divide responsibilities to show balanced teamwork and support?"*

5. *"What's one thing we could do this week to connect as a family?"*

6. **For Extended or Blended Families**

7. *"What unique strengths does each family member bring to the table, and how can we celebrate those?"*

8. *"How can we honor our family's cultural or generational heritage in a way that feels meaningful to everyone?"*

9. *"What's one family tradition we could start or revisit together?"*

10. **For Single Parent or Independent Youth Homes**

11. *"What household tasks do you feel ready to take responsibility for, and how can I support you?"*

12. *"What's one thing we can do together this week to make the house run more smoothly?"*

13. *"What skills would you like to learn that could help you feel more independent and confident?"*

14. Shared Ritual Ideas for Strengthening Connections

15. **General Ideas (Applicable to All Families)**

16. **Gratitude Jar**: Place a jar in a common area where family members can drop in notes about what they're grateful for. Read them together weekly.

17. **Family Playlist**: Create a shared music playlist where everyone adds their favorite songs. Use it during cooking or cleaning sessions.

18. **Story Circle**: Take turns sharing stories from the week or from family history during a meal or designated storytelling time.

19. **Two-Lead Adult Homes**

20. **Rotating Leadership**: Alternate who leads a family activity each week, such as planning a game night or choosing a weekend outing.

21. **Co-Parent Check-Ins**: Set aside 15 minutes weekly to align on family goals, responsibilities, and challenges.

22. Extended or Blended Families

23. **Cultural Potluck**: Host a monthly dinner where everyone

brings or helps prepare a dish tied to their cultural background.

24. **Generational Wisdom Night**: Invite elders to share life lessons or stories while younger members ask questions.

25. **Single Parent or Independent Youth Homes**

26. **Chore Challenge**: Turn household responsibilities into a friendly competition with small rewards for creativity or efficiency.

27. **Skill Swap Saturdays**: Dedicate time to teaching each other new skills, like fixing something, cooking, or using a new tool.

28. Task-Sharing Guide for Collaborative Homes

Goal: Delegate responsibilities effectively while teaching teens independence and life skills.

1. **Task Delegation Tips**

2. **Match Skills to Tasks**: Assign responsibilities that align with individual strengths or interests.

3. Example: If a teen enjoys organizing, they might manage meal planning or pantry arrangements.

4. **Offer Support Initially**: Demonstrate tasks a few times and provide constructive feedback to build confidence.

5. **Celebrate Contributions**: Acknowledge effort and improvements during family check-ins.

6. **Reflection Questions for Implementation**

7. *What shared ritual could bring the most value to our family right now?*

8. *How can we make task-sharing feel less like a chore and more like an opportunity for connection?*

9. *What conversation prompt can we use this week to spark meaningful dialogue at home?*

CONCLUSION

Further Reading and Research

The Maya Bechi Method™ (MBM) draws from a diverse range of disciplines, including child development, psychology, family studies, and cultural practices. Below is a curated list of recommended books, articles, and references that have informed and supported the MBM framework. These resources provide deeper insights into the principles underlying MBM, as well as practical strategies for families.

Recommended Books and Articles

Parenting and Adolescence

"The Whole-Brain Child" by Daniel J. Siegel and Tina Payne Bryson

- Explores how brain development impacts behavior and provides strategies to help parents nurture emotional resilience in their children.

"How to Raise an Adult" by Julie Lythcott-Haims

- Examines overparenting and offers practical advice on fostering independence and self-reliance in children and teens.

"Emotional Intelligence 2.0" by Travis Bradberry and Jean Greaves

- A practical guide to understanding and improving emotional intelligence, a key element in MBM's self-awareness focus.

"Grit: The Power of Passion and Perseverance" by Angela Duckworth

- Discusses the importance of persistence and how parents can foster this trait in their children.

Identity and Emotional Growth

"Identity Leadership" by Stedman Graham

- Explores the concept of identity as the foundation for personal leadership and offers actionable steps for self-awareness and growth.

"Raising Good Humans" by Hunter Clarke-Fields

- Focuses on mindful parenting techniques to cultivate kindness, responsibility, and emotional intelligence in children.

"The Gifts of Imperfection" by Brené Brown

- Encourages self-compassion and vulnerability, key aspects of fostering emotional resilience in both parents and teens.

Family and Cultural Dynamics

"Parenting with Love and Logic" by Charles Fay and Foster Cline

- Offers techniques for setting boundaries and allowing natural consequences to teach responsibility.

"Hold On to Your Kids: Why Parents Need to Matter More Than Peers" by Gordon Neufeld & Gabor Maté

- Highlights the importance of strong parent-child relationships in a world increasingly influenced by peers and technology.

1. Articles from Common Sense Media

- Various articles and resources on digital literacy, healthy screen habits, and fostering digital resilience in teens.

References and Evidence Supporting the MBM

Research and Studies

1. **American Psychological Association**

   - Articles on adolescent brain development, emotional intelligence, and the impact of family dynamics on teen behavior.

   - Source: www.apa.org

2. **Collaborative and Proactive Solutions (CPS) by Ross** W. Greene Framework for collaborative problem-solving with children and teens.

3. **Digital Literacy Research from Common Sense Media**

   - Studies on the effects of screen time and strategies for building digital resilience.

4. **Daniel Goleman's Work on Emotional Intelligence**

   - Foundational research on the importance of emotional intelligence for success and well-being.

5. **Montessori Education Principles**

   - Insights into pre-taught and experience learning, adapted for MBM's focus on adolescence.

6. **Journal of Family Psychology**

   - Research on family-based emotional interventions and the impact of co-participation on trust and emotional regulation.

MAYA BECHI

ABOUT THE AUTHOR

Maya Bechi is an educator, parent, and writer with a passion for helping families navigate the challenges of raising teens in a rapidly changing world. The inspiration for *Raising Reliable Rebels, the Maya Bechi Method*™ came from her personal journey as a newly divorced, co-parenting mother of two, desperately seeking credible and effective strategies to create a nurturing, balanced home environment. She is still imperfectly using the method in her home.

Maya's greatest achievement is her decision to re-evaluate and re-orient her family's home life during a decade marked by immense technological, emotional, spiritual, intellectual, and physical upheaval. With only the credentials of "mother" and an unyielding determination, she is sharing her notes and reflections via a transformative philosophy to guide parents through the complexities of modern parenting.

When she's not writing or sharing her method with other parents, Maya enjoys learning more about homesteading, attending live concerts, and enjoying time with family, friends and the outdoors.

https://www.robsonandpuritan.com
contact@robsonandpuritan.com

mbechi@recoupinternal.com